D1504064

DATE DUE

Regulating Violence
in Entertainment

Affirmative Action

Amateur Athletics

American Military Policy

Animal Rights

Bankruptcy Law

Blogging

Capital Punishment,
Second Edition

Disaster Relief

DNA Evidence

Educational Standards

Election Reform

Energy Policy

Environmental Regulations
and Global Warming

The FCC and Regulating
Indecency

Fetal Rights

Food Safety

Freedom of Speech

Gay Rights

Gun Control

Hate Crimes

Immigrants' Rights After 9/11

Immigration Policy,
Second Edition

The Internet and Crime

Juvenile Justice

Legalizing Marijuana

Mandatory Military Service

Media Bias

Mental Health Reform

Miranda Rights

Open Government

Physician-Assisted Suicide

Policing the Internet

Prescription and
Non-prescription Drugs

Prisoners' Rights

Private Property Rights

Product Liability

Protecting Ideas

Regulating Violence in
Entertainment

Religion in Public Schools

Reproductive Rights

The Right to Die

The Right to Privacy

Rights of Students

Search and Seizure

Smoking Bans, Second Edition

Stem Cell Research and Cloning

Tort Reform

Trial of Juveniles as Adults

Unions and Labor Laws

Universal Healthcare

The War on Terror,
Second Edition

Welfare Reform

White-Collar Crime

Women in the Military

Regulating Violence in Entertainment

Paul Ruschmann, J.D.

SERIES EDITOR
Alan Marzilli, M.A., J.D.

CHELSEA HOUSE
PUBLISHERS
An imprint of Infobase Publishing

Chelsea House
An imprint of Infobase Publishing
132 West 31st Street
New York, NY 10001

Library of Congress Cataloging-in-Publication Data

Ruschmann, Paul.
 Regulating violence in entertainment / by Paul Ruschmann.
 p. cm. — (Point/counterpoint)
 Includes bibliographical references and index.
 ISBN 978-1-60413-510-7 (hardcover)
 1. Violence in mass media—Law and legislation—United States—Juvenile literature.
2. Mass media—Law and legislation—United States—Juvenile literature. 3. Violence in mass media—Juvenile literature. I. Title.
 KF2750.R87 2010
 344.73'099—dc22
                          2009034813

Chelsea House books are available at special discounts when purchased in bulk quantities for businesses, associations, institutions, or sales promotions. Please call our Special Sales Department in New York at (212) 967-8800 or (800) 322-8755.

You can find Chelsea House on the World Wide Web at http://www.chelseahouse.com.

Text design by Keith Trego
Cover design by Alicia Post
Composition by EJB Publishing Services
Cover printed by Bang Printing, Brainerd, MN
Book printed and bound by Bang Printing, Brainerd, MN
Date printed: June 2010
Printed in the United States of America

10 9 8 7 6 5 4 3 2 1

This book is printed on acid-free paper.

All links and Web addresses were checked and verified to be correct at the time of publication. Because of the dynamic nature of the Web, some addresses and links may have changed since publication and may no longer be valid.

Foreword	6
INTRODUCTION	
Violence, Entertainment, and Society	11
POINT	
Violent Entertainment Is a Serious Problem	26
COUNTERPOINT	
The Dangers of Violent Entertainment Are Exaggerated	40
POINT	
The Entertainment Industry Has Acted Irresponsibly	54
COUNTERPOINT	
Critics Wrongly Blame Entertainment for Crime	70
POINT	
Regulating Entertainment Is Necessary	86
COUNTERPOINT	
Regulating Entertainment Is Bad Policy	101
CONCLUSION	
Looking Ahead	115
Appendix: Beginning Legal Research	130
Elements of the Argument	133
Notes	136
Resources	139
Picture Credits	143
Index	144

FOREWORD ||||▷

Alan Marzilli, M.A., J.D.
Birmingham, Alabama

The POINT/COUNTERPOINT series offers the reader a greater understanding of some of the most controversial issues in contemporary American society—issues such as capital punishment, immigration, gay rights, and gun control. We have looked for the most contemporary issues and have included topics—such as the controversies surrounding "blogging"—that we could not have imagined when the series began.

In each volume, the author has selected an issue of particular importance and set out some of the key arguments on both sides of the issue. Why study both sides of the debate? Maybe you have yet to make up your mind on an issue, and the arguments presented in the book will help you to form an opinion. More likely, however, you will already have an opinion on many of the issues covered by the series. There is always the chance that you will change your opinion after reading the arguments for the other side. But even if you are firmly committed to an issue—for example, school prayer or animal rights—reading both sides of the argument will help you to become a more effective advocate for your cause. By gaining an understanding of opposing arguments, you can develop answers to those arguments.

Perhaps more importantly, listening to the other side sometimes helps you see your opponent's arguments in a more human way. For example, Sister Helen Prejean, one of the nation's most visible opponents of capital punishment, has been deeply affected by her interactions with the families of murder victims. By seeing the families' grief and pain, she understands much better why people support the death penalty, and she is able to carry out her advocacy with a greater sensitivity to the needs and beliefs of death penalty supporters.

The books in the series include numerous features that help the reader to gain a greater understanding of the issues. Real-life examples illustrate the human side of the issues. Each chapter also includes excerpts from relevant laws, court cases, and other material, which provide a better foundation for understanding the arguments. The

6

volumes contain citations to relevant sources of law and information, and an appendix guides the reader through the basics of legal research, both on the Internet and in the library. Today, through free Web sites, it is easy to access legal documents, and these books might give you ideas for your own research.

Studying the issues covered by the POINT/COUNTERPOINT series is more than an academic activity. The issues described in the books affect all of us as citizens. They are the issues that today's leaders debate and tomorrow's leaders will decide. While all of the issues covered in the POINT/COUNTERPOINT series are controversial today, and will remain so for the foreseeable future, it is entirely possible that the reader might one day play a central role in resolving the debate. Today it might seem that some debates—such as capital punishment and abortion—will never be resolved.

However, our nation's history is full of debates that seemed as though they never would be resolved, and many of the issues are now well settled—at least on the surface. In the nineteenth century, abolitionists met with widespread resistance to their efforts to end slavery. Ultimately, the controversy threatened the union, leading to the Civil War between the northern and southern states. Today, while a public debate over the merits of slavery would be unthinkable, racism persists in many aspects of society.

Similarly, today nobody questions women's right to vote. Yet at the beginning of the twentieth century, suffragists fought public battles for women's voting rights, and it was not until the passage of the Nineteenth Amendment in 1920 that the legal right of women to vote was established nationwide.

What makes an issue controversial? Often, controversies arise when most people agree that there is a problem but disagree about the best way to solve it. There is little argument that poverty is a major problem in the United States, especially in inner cities and rural areas. Yet, people disagree vehemently about the best way to address the problem. To some, the answer is social programs, such as welfare, food stamps, and public housing. However, many argue that such subsidies encourage dependence on government benefits while unfairly penalizing those who work and pay taxes, and that the real solution is to require people to support themselves.

American society is in a constant state of change, and sometimes modern practices clash with what many consider to be "traditional values," which are often rooted in conservative political views or religious beliefs. Many blame high crime rates, and problems such as poverty, illiteracy, and drug use on the breakdown of the traditional family structure of a married mother and father raising their children. Since the "sexual revolution" of the 1960s and 1970s, sparked in part by the widespread availability of the birth control pill, marriage rates have declined, and the number of children born outside of marriage has increased. The sexual revolution led to controversies over birth control, sex education, and other issues, most prominently abortion. Similarly, the gay rights movement has been challenged as a threat to traditional values. While many gay men and lesbians want to have the same right to marry and raise families as heterosexuals, many politicians and others have challenged gay marriage and adoption as a threat to American society.

Sometimes, new technology raises issues that we have never faced before, and society disagrees about the best solution. Are people free to swap music online, or does this violate the copyright laws that protect songwriters and musicians' ownership of the music that they create? Should scientists use "genetic engineering" to create new crops that are resistant to disease and pests and produce more food, or is it too risky to use a laboratory to create plants that nature never intended? Modern medicine has continued to increase the average lifespan—which is now 77 years, up from under 50 years at the beginning of the twentieth century—but many people are now choosing to die in comfort rather than living with painful ailments in their later years. For doctors, this presents an ethical dilemma: should they allow their patients to die? Should they assist patients in ending their own lives painlessly?

Perhaps the most controversial issues are those that implicate a Constitutional right. The Bill of Rights—the first 10 Amendments to the U.S. Constitution—spells out some of the most fundamental rights that distinguish our democracy from other nations with fewer freedoms. However, the sparsely worded document is open to interpretation, with each side saying that the Constitution is on their side. The Bill of Rights was meant to protect individual liberties; however, the needs of some individuals clash with society's needs. Thus, the Constitution often serves as a battleground between individuals and government officials seeking to protect society in some way. The First Amendment's guarantee of "freedom of speech" leads to some very difficult questions. Some forms of expression—such as burning an American flag—lead to public outrage, but are protected by the First Amendment. Other types of expression that most people find objectionable—such as child pornography—are not protected by the Constitution. The question is not only where to draw the line, but whether drawing lines around constitutional rights threatens our liberty.

The Bill of Rights raises many other questions about individual rights and societal "good." Is a prayer before a high school football game an "establishment of religion" prohibited by the First Amendment? Does the Second Amendment's promise of "the right to bear arms" include concealed handguns? Does stopping and frisking someone standing on a known drug corner constitute "unreasonable search and seizure" in violation of the Fourth Amendment? Although the U.S. Supreme Court has the ultimate authority in interpreting the U.S. Constitution, its answers do not always satisfy the public. When a group of nine people—sometimes by a five-to-four vote—makes a decision that affects hundreds of millions of others, public outcry can be expected. For example, the Supreme Court's 1973 ruling in *Roe v. Wade* that abortion is protected by the Constitution did little to quell the debate over abortion.

Whatever the root of the controversy, the books in the POINT/ COUNTERPOINT series seek to explain to the reader the origins of the debate, the current state of the law, and the arguments on either side of the debate. Our hope in creating this series is that readers will be better informed about the issues facing not only our politicians, but all of our nation's citizens, and become more actively involved in resolving these debates, as voters, concerned citizens, journalists, or maybe even elected officials.

Whenever a Constitutional issue of free speech is debated, passions often run high. When a powerful industry is involved in the debate, it can become even more heated. After enjoying several decades relatively free from interference, the entertainment industry is finding itself increasingly under attack—not just for sexually suggestive entertainment, but also for graphic portrayals of violence. Critics of the violence that can be seen regularly on television, in movies, and in video games point to academic studies suggesting links between viewing dramatized violence and committing violent acts. Defenders of the industry, as well as supporters of free speech, question these studies, suggesting that other factors explain youth violence. They say that the industry's efforts, such as voluntary movie and video game ratings, help parents protect their children from material they find objectionable. Parents' groups and other concerned citizens counter that such measures are ineffective and that binding legal restrictions are necessary. This volume examines these and other arguments in its exploration of whether violence in entertainment is indeed a problem facing American society, and, if so, what can be done about it.

Violence, Entertainment, and Society

On April 20, 1999, students Eric Harris and Dylan Klebold entered Columbine High School armed with semiautomatic weapons and handguns. They killed 12 students and a teacher and wounded 24 other people before fatally shooting themselves. Experts offered a number of explanations for the attack. Some, such as psychologists Craig A. Anderson and Karen Dill, said that video games played a large role:

> Harris and Klebold enjoyed playing the bloody, shoot-'em-up video game *Doom*, a game licensed by the U.S. military to train soldiers to effectively kill. . . . For a class project, Harris and Klebold made a videotape that was similar to their customized version of *Doom*. In the video, Harris and Klebold dress in trench coats, carry

guns, and kill school athletes. They acted out their videotaped performance in real life less than a year later. [1]

Many Americans blamed violent entertainment for the
shootings. A *Time*-CNN survey taken shortly after the Columbine
massacre found that a majority of teenagers and adults blamed
the media. Lawmakers in Congress introduced a number of bills
aimed at keeping violent entertainment away from young people.
Hillary Rodham Clinton, who was then First Lady, asked, "What
kind of values are we promoting . . . when a child can walk into
a store and find video games where you win based on how many
people you can kill or how many places you can blow up?"[2] The
issue of violent entertainment was even raised during the 2000
presidential campaign.

The debate over violent entertainment raises several important questions. First, does exposure to such entertainment lead to
real-world violence? Second, is violent entertainment so harmful that government should regulate it? Finally, does the U.S.
Constitution stand in the way of regulation?

The First Amendment and Entertainment

Our government's authority to regulate violent entertainment is
limited by the First Amendment to the U.S. Constitution, which
provides: "Congress shall make no law respecting an establishment of religion, or prohibiting the free exercise thereof; or
abridging the freedom of speech, or of the press; or the right of
the people peaceably to assemble, and to petition the government for a redress of grievances."[3] For many years, the First
Amendment offered little protection to the entertainment industry because the U.S. Supreme Court ruled that it applied only
to political speech. For example, in 1915 the Court rendered an
opinion that upheld an Ohio censorship law giving a state board
power to decide which films could legally be shown: "It cannot
be put out of view that the exhibition of moving pictures is a
business, pure and simple, originated and conducted for profit,

A detail of the Columbine High School class photo of the Class of 1999. Pictured in the top row (*from left*) are Eric Harris and Dylan Klebold, who killed 12 students and one teacher at the school on April 20, 1999. Harris and Klebold also injured 21 other students directly before committing suicide. According to reports, the pair was inspired to commit this crime because of violent entertainment.

like other spectacles, not to be regarded, nor intended to be regarded . . . as part of the press of the country, or as organs of public opinion."[4]

In the mid-twentieth century, the Supreme Court extended First Amendment protection to entertainment. In the 1948 case of *Winters v. New York*, the justices overturned a New York law banning "true crime" magazines because it was too vague. In doing so, they said, "The line between the informing and the entertaining is too elusive for the protection of that basic [First Amendment] right. . . . What is one man's amusement, teaches another's doctrine."[5] Four years later, in *Joseph Burstyn, Inc. v. Wilson*, the Court said:

> It cannot be doubted that motion pictures are a significant medium for the communication of ideas. They may affect public attitudes and behavior in a variety of ways, ranging from direct espousal of a political or social doctrine to the subtle shaping of thought which characterizes all artistic expression. The importance of motion pictures as an organ of public opinion is not lessened by the fact that they are designed to entertain as well as to inform.[6]

Although the First Amendment protects entertainment, there are limits to that protection. Obscenity has always been considered unprotected speech. Nowadays we associate the term *obscenity* with sex, but that term once applied to other material, including depictions of violence. In the late nineteenth century, for example, antiobscenity crusader Anthony Comstock persuaded the New York legislature to pass an obscenity law that banned publications "principally made up of criminal news, police reports, or accounts of criminal deeds, or pictures, or stories of deeds of bloodshed, lust, or crime."[7] Many other states passed similar laws. Legislators believed that these laws protected vulnerable people, especially the young, from the corrupting influence of popular culture. Our courts upheld these laws. In doing so, they followed the reasoning of an 1868 British decision, *The Queen v. Hicklin*, under which the government could ban a work if it contained material that tended to corrupt the most susceptible members of society. Thus, a work could be placed off-limits, even for adults, if a judge found that it had a harmful effect on young people. In fact, a single offending passage was enough to condemn an entire work.

In the mid-twentieth century, the Supreme Court began to draw a line between protected speech and obscenity. In the 1957 case of *Butler v. Michigan*, the Court rejected the *Hicklin* standard, ruling that the government could no longer ban the sale of a book to adults on the grounds that it was harmful to young readers. In *Roth v. United States*, also a 1957 case, the Court ruled that works with serious social value were not obscene. Sixteen years later, the justices decided *Miller v. California*, which laid down a three-part test for obscenity:

> (a) whether "the average person, applying contemporary community standards" would find that the work, taken as a whole, appeals to the prurient interest; (b) whether the work depicts or describes, in a patently offensive way, sexual conduct specifically defined by the applicable state law; and (c) whether the work, taken as a whole, lacks serious literary, artistic, political, or scientific value.[8]

Material that is "harmful to minors"—obscene for young people but not adults—has a lower level of First Amendment protection. Even after the *Roth* decision, lawmakers assumed that the Court would give them greater leeway to keep pornographic material away from young people. In the 1968 case of *Ginsberg v. New York*, the justices concluded that the state could set a minimum age for buying material defined as harmful to minors. *Ginsberg* remains the law today. The government can impose greater restrictions on young people's access to sexual material than it can for adults' access.

Although the *Miller* and *Ginsberg* decisions dealt with material of a sexual nature, some advocates insist that graphic depictions of violence—especially those found in entertainment—can be so offensive that they belong in the "harmful to minors" category and, in extreme cases, could fall within the definition of obscenity. The U.S. Supreme Court has not yet addressed this argument.

Radio and television also enjoy a lower level of First Amendment protection. Since its earliest days, the Federal Communications Commission (FCC) has heavily regulated the broadcasting industry. Broadcasters required a license from the FCC to operate a station, and the FCC had broad power to regulate what went on the air by fining violators and, in extreme cases, taking away their licenses. Today, stations must follow the Broadcast Decency Rule, which requires them to confine "indecent" radio and television programs to the hours of 10 P.M. to 6 A.M., when relatively few young people are in the audience. The FCC defines indecent programming as "language or material that, in context, depicts or describes, in terms patently offensive as measured by contemporary community standards for the broadcast medium, sexual or excretory activities or organs."[9] In 1978, the Supreme Court affirmed the Broadcast Decency Rule in *Federal Communications Commission v. Pacifica Foundation.* Some advocacy groups argue that the rule should be extended to violence, which in their view is also harmful to young audiences. The FCC agrees with that position, but neither it nor Congress has tried to extend the rule to violence.

Criticism and Industry Self-Regulation

The law is not the only restraint on the entertainment industry. Public opinion is also a powerful influence. Critics have complained about offensive entertainment as least as far back as 1740. In that year, they accused Samuel Richardson's *Pamela,* one of the first English-language novels, of corrupting the young.

Also in the nineteenth century, critics contended that "dime novels"—paperbound adventure stories popular with young readers—made readers more prone to crime and delinquency. When motion pictures arrived, they, too, were met with criticism. When *The Great Train Robbery*, one of the earliest silent films,

FROM THE BENCH

Roth v. United States, 354 U.S. 476 (1957) and Miller v. California, 413 U.S. 15, 24 (1973)

Some advocates contend that violent entertainment should be treated as a form of obscenity, a category of speech that has always been outside the protection of the First Amendment. At the time the Bill of Rights was adopted, every state had a law against blasphemy or profanity, out of which obscenity laws evolved. In *Roth v. United States*, the U.S. Supreme Court said that the test for obscene material was "whether to the average person, applying contemporary community standards, the dominant theme of the material taken as a whole appeals to prurient interest" and whether it was "utterly without redeeming social importance."

Roth did not settle the issue of what was obscene. The justices struggled with that issue for 16 more years until the Court decided *Miller v. California*. In that case, the Court announced a three-part test, as mentioned earlier: "(a) whether 'the average person, applying contemporary community standards' would find that the work, taken as a whole, appeals to the prurient interest; (b) whether the work depicts or describes, in a patently offensive way, sexual conduct specifically defined by the applicable state law; and (c) whether the work, taken as a whole, lacks serious literary, artistic, political, or scientific value." The first, or "community standards," portion of this test recognizes that some parts of the country are more conservative than others. However, the third, or "serious . . . value," portion establishes a "nationwide floor" of First Amendment protection. Material with serious social value is not obscene, no matter how offensive it may be to members of a local community.

The *Miller* case dealt with material of a sexual nature, but supporters of laws regulating violent entertainment insist that obscenity is not limited to sexual depictions. They point out that the basis of obscenity is offensiveness, and that some depictions of extreme violence are so offensive to society that they fall outside the protection of the First Amendment.

debuted in 1903, it was criticized for its violent content, despite being only 12 minutes long. Soon after the film was shown, critics blamed it for a real-life train robbery in Pennsylvania.

Critics have also aired their complaints in public forums, including Congress and state legislatures. The result has often been self-regulation by the entertainment industry. In 1909, the motion picture industry created a censorship board called the National Board of Review. In the 1930s, it adopted the stringent "Hays Code," which dictated what Americans saw in theaters. Researchers Lawrence Kutner and Cheryl K. Olson explain the motivation for self-censorship:

> The film industry's attempt at setting moral standards for motion pictures was fundamentally a business decision, an attempt to ward off costly distribution problems if state governments developed different standards for what could be shown in their theaters. It was an approach that would later be copied by the creators of other entertainment media, including video games.[10]

In the 1960s, the Hays Code gave way to a system of age-based ratings. Not only does this ratings system still exist, but it is also a model for self-regulation elsewhere in the entertainment industry.

Motion pictures were not the only target of critics. In 1954, the prominent psychiatrist Fredric Wertham wrote *Seduction of the Innocent*, in which he argued that comic books were a cause of juvenile delinquency. Wertham told a Senate panel investigating comic books: "If it were my task, Mr. Chairman, to teach children delinquency, to tell them how to rape and seduce girls, how to hurt people, how to break into stores, how to cheat, how to forge, how to do any known crime—if it were my task to do that, I would have to enlist the crime comic book industry."[11] The industry reacted by adopting a new code that directed publishers not to glorify crime, depict excessive violence, or even draw suggestive-looking characters.

During the 1950s, millions of Americans bought television sets for the first time. At the same time, Congress began to investigate what programs were being shown to Americans. Violence was one topic of interest. Like the motion picture industry, broadcasters decided to regulate themselves. In 1952, the National Association of Broadcasters adopted the Television Code, which emphasized broadcasters' responsibility toward the public, especially young viewers, and spelled out a long list of unacceptable practices. The code survived until the early 1980s, when the industry abandoned it after the federal government challenged portions of it as an illegal restraint of trade. Violence on television has continued to be a concern of lawmakers. In 1996, Congress passed a law that required manufacturers to equip television sets with a "V-chip," a device that allows parents to block programs they consider inappropriate. That same legislation also forced the broadcast industry to create a rating system. Even though the V-chip is widely available, a 2004 survey by the Kaiser Family Foundation found that only 15 percent of parents had used the device.

In the 1950s, researchers began to study whether there was a link between watching violent television and committing real-world acts of violence. By 1976, there was enough evidence of such a link that the American Medical Association (AMA) passed a resolution stating: "The [AMA] House [of Delegates] declares TV violence threatens the health and welfare of young Americans, commits itself to remedial actions with interested parties, and encourages opposition to TV programs containing violence and to their sponsors."[12] Researchers later expanded their investigation to other media and found that those media, too, could harm young people.

The Age of New Media Arrives

During the 1970s and 1980s, a variety of new media arrived, which many Americans considered harmful to young people. Music lyrics had become more explicit, and critics argued that they encouraged young listeners to engage in antisocial behavior. Adding to the controversy was the use of music videos to promote new songs. Some videos were criticized for sexual content and for glorifying violence and the use of weapons. In 1984, a group of activists led by Tipper Gore, the wife of Senator Al Gore (who would later serve as vice president under President Bill Clinton), formed an advocacy group called the Parents Music Resource Center. Its efforts led recording companies to place "Parental Advisory" labels on any packages of recorded music containing lyrics glorifying violence, sexual activity, or substance abuse, or containing profane language.

By the 1990s, video game technology had advanced to the point that some games offered a sophisticated form of

FROM THE BENCH

Ginsberg v. New York, 390 U.S. 629 (1968)

Supporters of regulation often refer to violent entertainment as "harmful to minors." That phrase has a specific meaning in the law. It was originally used to refer to pornography that is not legally obscene but is nevertheless considered damaging to teenagers who view it. The harmful-to-minors doctrine is an outgrowth of obscenity law.

In *Ginsberg v. New York*, the Supreme Court ruled that the government could apply a different standard of obscenity for young people than it uses for adults. That case began when a store owner, Sam Ginsberg, sold two magazines containing photographs of naked women to a person younger than 17, the minimum age in New York State for buying materials defined as "harmful to minors." Ginsberg was convicted of violating the law but argued on appeal that the law was unconstitutional.

Ginsberg's appeal eventually reached the Supreme Court, which upheld the conviction. Justice William Brennan wrote the Court's decision. He first upheld the concept of "variable obscenity": In other words, what was obscene depended on the group of people to which it was directed. Young people were one such group. Brennan said that the state had two justifications for passing harmful-to-minors laws. First, they helped parents raise their children properly:

virtual reality. When the games became popular, parents became concerned that playing them affected their children's minds. Congress investigated the video game industry after violent games such as *Doom* and *Mortal Kombat* went on sale. In 1994, the video game industry created the Entertainment Software Rating Board (ESRB), which instituted a system of self-regulation that includes ratings.

In 2000, a group of leading public-health organizations issued a statement pertaining to violent entertainment in which they said, "[T]here is a strong consensus on many of the effects on children's health, well-being, and development," and "[t]he conclusion of the public health community, based on over 30 years of research, is that viewing entertainment violence can

"The legislature could properly conclude that parents and others, teachers for example, who have this primary responsibility for children's well-being are entitled to the support of laws designed to aid discharge of that responsibility." Second, the state had an independent interest in the well being of its young people. Brennan quoted from another New York obscenity decision: "While the supervision of children's reading may best be left to their parents, the knowledge that parental control or guidance cannot always be provided and society's transcendent interest in protecting the welfare of children justify reasonable regulation of the sale of material to them."

A significant aspect of the *Ginsberg* decision is that the Court applied a "rational-basis" standard, a low level of scrutiny under which it deferred to New York lawmakers' determination that pornography was harmful to young people and that setting an age limit for purchase was an appropriate way to protect them from harm. In fact, Justice Brennan accepted New York's assertion that pornography was harmful without demanding scientific proof.

After the Supreme Court decided *Miller v. California* in 1973, states amended their harmful-to-minors laws to incorporate the three-part *Miller* test. Those laws define "prurient interest" and "patently offensive" with respect to those under a given age, usually 17 or 18.

lead to increases in aggressive attitudes, values, and behavior, particularly in children."[13] That same year, the president of the American Academy of Pediatrics told a Senate committee:

> Since the 1950s, more than 3,500 research studies in the United States and around the world using many investigative methods have examined whether there is an association between exposure to media violence and subsequent violent behavior. All but 18 have shown a positive correlation between media exposure and violent behavior.[14]

FROM THE BENCH

Winters v. New York, 333 U.S. 507 (1948)

Section 1141(2) of the New York Penal Law provided that any person who prints, publishes, or distributes "any book, pamphlet, magazine, newspaper, or other printed paper devoted to the publication, and principally made up of criminal news, police reports, or accounts of criminal deeds, or pictures, or stories of deeds of bloodshed, lust or crime" was guilty of a misdemeanor.

Murray Winters, a bookseller in New York City, was convicted of violating that law by selling copies of *Headquarters Detective*, a "true crime" publication filled with detailed descriptions of violent crimes. His appeal reached the U.S. Supreme Court. In *Winters v. New York*, a six-to-three majority of the justices found the law unconstitutional and reversed Winters's conviction.

Writing for the majority, Justice Stanley Reed said that the First Amendment was not limited to the exposition of ideas:

> The line between the informing and the entertaining is too elusive for the protection of that basic right. Everyone is familiar with instances of propaganda through fiction. What is one man's amusement, teaches another's doctrine. Though we can see nothing of any possible value to society in these magazines, they are as much entitled to the protection of free speech as the best of literature.

Justice Reed next concluded that the law failed to give fair warning of what was prohibited. He alluded to "the utter impossibility of the actor or the trier to know

Regulation and Legal Challenges

As policy makers became more concerned about entertainment, the Supreme Court expanded its First Amendment protection. Because constitutionally protected speech was involved, the Court required laws regulating that speech to meet a very high standard:

> We have recognized that there is a compelling interest in protecting the physical and psychological well-being of minors. . . . The Government may serve this legitimate interest, but to withstand constitutional scrutiny, it must

where this new standard of guilt would draw the line between the allowable and the forbidden publications."

In his dissenting opinion, Justice Felix Frankfurter wrote: "This body of laws represents but one of the many attempts by legislatures to solve what is perhaps the most persistent, intractable, elusive, and demanding of all problems of society—the problem of crime, and, more particularly, of its prevention." Frankfurter added that courts should defer to state lawmakers' determination of what might cause crime because complex questions of individual and social behavior were involved. He further argued that publications like *Headquarters Detective* not only lacked social value but also were harmful to society and accused the majority of turning a blind eye to that harm. Finally, Frankfurter expressed his frustration with the majority's conclusion that the law was too vague:

> What standard of definiteness does the Court furnish the New York legislature in finding indefiniteness in the present law? Should the New York legislature enumerate by name the publications which in its judgment are "inciting violent and depraved crimes"? Should the New York legislature spell out in detail the ingredients of stories or pictures which accomplish such "inciting"? What is there in the condemned law that leaves men in the dark as to what is meant by publications that exploit "criminal deeds of bloodshed or lust" thereby "inciting violent and depraved crimes"?

do so by narrowly drawn regulations designed to serve those interests without unnecessarily interfering with First Amendment freedoms. It is not enough to show that the Government's ends are compelling; the means must be carefully tailored to achieve those ends.[15]

The so-called strict-scrutiny standard makes it very difficult for the government to regulate entertainment, even for the purpose of protecting young people. One example is the battle over Internet pornography. In 1996, after the media reported that online pornography was easily available, Congress passed the Communications Decency Act (CDA), which required Web site owners who posted indecent content to make sure that users younger than 17 could not access it. In *Reno v. American Civil Liberties Union* (1997), the Supreme Court overturned that law because its definition of "indecent" was too vague. Congress responded by passing a narrower law called the Child Online Protection Act (COPA). That was also found to be too restrictive of speech.

The current legal battleground involves video games. In recent years, a number of states have passed laws banning retailers from selling violent games to customers younger than 18. So far, not one of these laws has been found constitutional. The courts have ruled that video games are a form of speech protected by the First Amendment. They have also concluded that existing studies are not convincing evidence that playing violent video games can lead to real-world violence.

Summary

Tragedies like the shootings at Columbine focused attention on the link between violent entertainment and crime. Many Americans have called for laws that would protect young people from such entertainment. Even though their arguments are similar to those made years ago against other forms of entertainment, critics believe the case for regulation has grown stronger.

They point to scientific evidence showing that exposure to violent entertainment at an early age leads to real-world violence later on. Because the First Amendment protects entertainment as free speech, however, the courts apply a demanding standard of review to laws regulating access to it. The courts recognize society's interest in protecting young people but so far have not ruled that laws regulating indecency and pornography apply to violent entertainment as well.

Violent Entertainment Is a Serious Problem

I n 2005, the state of Texas executed Ronald Ray Howard for
fatally shooting a state trooper. According to the Texas Execution Information Center:

> Howard and his trial attorney said that his behavior
> was prompted in part by violent, antipolice rap music.
> Howard told a grand jury that he was listening to
> "Soulja's Story" by Tupac Shakur before the shoot-
> ing. The lyrics describe an African-American teenager
> shooting a police officer after being pulled over. In an
> interview on death row, Howard commented on the
> role that rap might have played in the murder: "I'm
> not a psychologist, . . . so I don't know. I never said, 'yes
> it did' or 'no it didn't.' I don't know. But my lawyers
> thought it could have caused it. And they were trying to
> justify, put reason for what I did.[1]

Cases like Howard's are becoming more common. Some argue that they provide support for research that shows a link between exposure to violent entertainment and violent acts in real life.

Entertainment is pervasive.

In 2000, the American Academy of Pediatrics found that Americans ages 2 to 18 spend on average more than six and a half hours a day using media of all kinds. That is more time than they spend on any other activity, except sleeping. It is easy to spend so much time with media because of its availability. In 1999, a U.S. Senate panel found that a large majority of American households not only had at least one television set but also had a variety of other media such as a videocassette recorder (VCR), video game equipment, or a personal computer. Parents often fail to supervise young people's use of these media. A more recent study found that 81 percent of two- to seven-year-olds sometimes watched television without an adult present, and 70 to 91 percent of four- to six-year-olds had turned on the television by themselves.

These same young people who consume hours of media find themselves at risk of being the victims of violence. According to the American Academy of Pediatrics:

> Homicide, suicide, and trauma are leading causes of mortality in the pediatric population. . . . Among urban youth, interpersonal violence is the most prevalent cause of injury (33%), and the incidence of gunshot wounds has increased dramatically in the past decade. Gun violence is now a leading killer of children and adolescents. Each year, 3,500 adolescents are murdered and more than 150,000 adolescents are arrested for violent crimes.[2]

Critics of the entertainment industry point out that high levels of violent crime have coincided with high levels of violence in the media. By age 18, the average person has seen an estimated 200,000 acts of violence—including 16,000 homicides—on television. The National Television Violence Study, which took place in the mid-1990s, found that three to five violent acts occur per hour during prime time and that children's television is even more violent, with 20 to 25 violent acts per hour during Saturday morning shows. Kevin W. Saunders, a law professor at Michigan State University, notes, "The broadcast media become no less pervasive in American life when violence rather than sex is involved. Similarly, the broadcast of violent material, just like the broadcast of sexual material, confronts the individual not only in public, but in the privacy of his or her own home."[3]

Entertainment influences behavior.

Many believe that the younger a person is, the more he or she will be negatively influenced by violent entertainment. Dr. Brandon Centerwall, who has studied violent television for years, argues that a small child cannot distinguish real life from fantasy, even with the help of adults. As a result, the child sees television as a factual source of information about the world outside. That world is not only violent, but also one in which violence has powerful emotional appeal. As a result, heavy watchers of violent television are more likely to act violently in the face of stressful moments later in life.

Because they cannot distinguish fantasy from reality, children often draw the wrong conclusions from the entertainment they watch. The National Television Violence Study found that nearly 75 percent of violent scenes featured no immediate punishment or condemnation for violence and that almost 45 percent of programs featured "bad" characters who rarely, if ever, got punished for their violent actions. In addition, studies show that the entertainment industry glamorizes violence—for example, making a hero of a gun-toting character—or sanitizes it by failing to show the suffering that results from violent acts. The American Academy of Pediatrics explains:

> Serious explorations of violence in plays like *Macbeth* and films like *Saving Private Ryan* treat violence as what it is—a human behavior that causes suffering, loss, and sadness to victims and perpetrators. In this context, viewers learn the danger and harm of violence by vicariously experiencing its outcomes. Unfortunately, most entertainment violence is used for immediate visceral thrills without portraying any human cost.[4]

Furthermore, young people learn by imitating characters they see on television, which sometimes causes them to hurt themselves or others. Young children have been injured while imitating professional wrestlers and martial-arts heroes, and teenagers have hurt themselves while performing stunts in hopes of being shown on the MTV show *Jackass*. In extreme cases, young people have killed others while imitating what they saw in the media. For example, Michael Carneal, who fatally shot three classmates at his high school in West Paducah, Kentucky, in 1997, had watched *The Basketball Diaries*, a film that contains a dream scene in which a character carries out a mass shooting as his school.

Studies link violent entertainment to real-world violence.

In 2000, six medical organizations issued a statement that said:

> At this time, well over 1,000 studies—including reports from the Surgeon General's office, the National Institute of Mental Health, and numerous studies conducted by leading figures within our medical and public health organizations—our own members—point overwhelmingly to a causal connection between media violence and aggressive behavior in some children.[5]

Researchers have a number of methods to measure the effects of exposure to violent entertainment. One is a laboratory experiment, in which researchers compare the behavior of children who are randomly assigned to watch a violent program with those who are randomly assigned to watch a nonviolent program. These studies generally measure short-term effects, such as increased hostility toward others.

Some researchers conduct longitudinal studies, which observe the behavior of a group of individuals over time, some-

The Columbia County Longitudinal Study

One way in which researchers measure the effects of violent entertainment is through a *longitudinal study*, which involves repeated observations over long periods of time. One such study is the Columbia County Longitudinal Study, pioneered by psychologist Leonard Eron. Dr. Eron and his colleagues went to Columbia County in upstate New York to investigate the factors that led children to act more aggressively later in life. Eron's team interviewed more than 850 third graders, as well as their parents, who identified the television programs their children watched. They also asked the participants' peers about threats, pushing, and other aggressive behavior. In 1963, they published the results of their study. One finding was that among boys there was a link between watching violent television at home and aggressive behavior at school.

Seven years later, the U.S. Surgeon General's Office, which was interested in the link between violent television and real-world violence, asked Eron and his colleagues to return to Columbia County. They found about half of the original study participants, who were now 19 years old, and interviewed them again. Based on those interviews, they found that boys who had watched violent television in third grade were more likely to get in trouble with the law as teenagers. Eron's team estimated that a preference for watching violent television in third grade might account for about 10 percent of the childhood influences that led boys to become aggressive as men.

In the early 1980s, Professor L. Rowell Huesmann and his colleagues went back to Columbia County for another follow-up. They located about half of the

times over a period of many years. Psychologist Leonard Eron conducted one such study, involving what children watch on television. In 1960, he interviewed a group of third graders in upstate New York and found a correlation between aggressive behavior in boys and their preference for violent television programs. Eron and his colleagues interviewed the same boys when they were 19 years old and again found a link between watching violent television in third grade and aggression as young adults. Eron's colleagues interviewed the participants

males from the original group, who were now 30 years old. They found "a strong relation between early violence viewing and later adult criminality." Participants who watched more violent television in third grade were also more likely as adults to use violence to discipline their children and to act aggressively toward their wives. In 1986, Huesmann reported his team's findings to the U.S. Senate Judiciary Committee, which was investigating violent television. Some observers credit Huesmann's work for the 1996 law that requires television sets to be equipped with a V-chip.

Journalist Richard Rhodes disputed the main finding of Eron's study. Rhodes pointed out that its main conclusion was based on a correlation between participants' preference for violent television as third graders and aggressiveness as reported by their peers, but the study found no correlation between preference for violent television and either aggression reported by the participants themselves or the results of psychological tests given to them. Nor did the study find any correlation for girls by any of the three measures. Rhodes argued that another team of researchers, looking at the same data, could have reached a different conclusion: Since only one of six possible correlations turned out to be significant, and that one correlation was relatively weak, the data did not link watching violent television to violent behavior later in life. Rhodes also argued that the link between childhood preference for violent television and a greater risk of criminal behavior later on was based on a tiny sample. Only three boys, out of a total of 145, were actually convicted of a crime. Huesmann himself acknowledged, "If just these three boys had behaved differently, all the significant results could have vanished."

Source: Richard Rhodes, "The Media Violence Myth," *Rolling Stone*, November 23, 2000.

once more when they were 30 years old. This time, they found an association between watching violent television as a child and committing violent crimes later in life.

Another well-known study by Dr. Centerwall focused on the long-term effects of exposure to television. He found that, in the United States and Canada, the homicide rate roughly doubled after television became commonplace, with a lag of 10 to 15 years between the introduction of television and the doubling of the homicide rate. Those findings were confirmed by what happened in South Africa, where television was not available until 1975. That country's homicide rate more than doubled in a little more than a decade after television arrived. Centerwall believes that television is so powerful an influence that "if, hypothetically, television technology had never been developed, there would today be 10,000 fewer homicides each year in the United States, 70,000 fewer rapes, and 700,000 fewer injurious assaults."[6]

Forty years of research into the effects of violent entertainment, especially on television, have convinced the public health community that there is a relationship between exposure to violent entertainment and real-life acts of violence. There are several reasons why this relationship exists:

- Violent entertainment sends a message that violence is normal and acceptable behavior. Some experts warn that a society that allows itself to become saturated with violence indirectly contributes to violence among some of its citizens.
- People exposed to violence become desensitized to it. Desensitized people are less likely to notice aggressive events, downplay the seriousness of the effects of violence, and feel less sympathy for victims of violence. They are also more tolerant of violence.
- Watching large amounts of violent entertainment leads to the "mean world" syndrome. The viewer not only

overestimates the amount of violence in the world outside, but also overreacts by distrusting others, carrying a
weapon, and even taking pre-emptive aggressive action.

Violent entertainment endangers public health.
We normally associate "public health" with diseases such as cancer and AIDS. There are, however, other threats to our health,
including pollution, traffic crashes, and violent crime. Often, the
government has stepped in to protect citizens from these threats.
Many Americans believe that the government should take steps
to protect young people from the effects of violent entertainment. The medical community has concluded that watching
violent entertainment can increase aggressive attitudes, values,
and behavior, especially in young people. In fact, the American
Academy of Pediatrics has concluded:

> The strength of the correlation . . . is greater than that of
> calcium intake and bone mass, lead ingestion and lower
> IQ, condom non-use and sexually acquired human
> immunodeficiency virus infection, or environmental
> tobacco smoke and lung cancer—associations clini-
> cians accept and on which preventive medicine is based
> without question.[7]

The academy believes that reducing young people's exposure to
it is as important as bicycle helmets, immunizations, and proper
nutrition.

Many scientists liken violent entertainment to another public health problem, tobacco use. The long-term effects of violent
entertainment, like those of cigarettes, increase with exposure. In
1999, Professor L. Rowell Huesmann, who has studied the effect
of violent media on young audiences, told a Senate committee:

> Not every child who watches a lot of violence or plays a lot
> of violent games will grow up to be violent. Other forces

must converge, as they did recently in [Columbine]. But just as every cigarette increases the chance that you will get lung cancer, every exposure to violence increases the chances that someday a child will behave more violently than they otherwise would.[8]

Does Watching Television Cause Violence? The Centerwall Study

Brandon Centerwall, a medical doctor, studied the relationship between exposure to violent television during childhood and violent crime later in life. Centerwall started with the premise that children learn by imitating what they see, including violence on television. In 1992, he published his findings in the *Journal of the American Medical Association*:

> [U]p through ages 3 and 4 years, many children are unable to distinguish fact from fantasy in television programs and remain unable to do so despite adult coaching. In the minds of such young children, television is a source of entirely factual information regarding how the world works. Naturally, as they get older, they come to know better, but the earliest and deepest impressions were laid down when the child saw television as a factual source of information about a world outside their homes where violence is a daily commonplace and the commission of violence is generally powerful, exciting, charismatic, and efficacious.

If Centerwall's assertion was correct, such violence would eventually show up in crime statistics. Centerwall tracked homicide rates in three countries—the United States, Canada, and South Africa—starting from when television was introduced in those countries. He found that, after the introduction of television in the United States, the homicide rate increased by 93 percent, from 3.0 per 100,000 residents in 1945 to 5.8 per 100,000 in 1974. In Canada, the homicide rate increased by 92 percent, from 1.3 per 100,000 residents in 1945 to 2.5 per 100,000 in 1974. In South Africa, the homicide rate in 1974, the year before the government allowed television, was 2.7 per 100,000. Twelve years later, that country's homicide rate was 130 percent higher.

Some also contend that violent entertainment, like tobacco, is addictive. Lieutenant Colonel Dave Grossman, a former psychology professor at the U.S. Military Academy, remarked: "Violence is like the nicotine in cigarettes.... The reason why the media has to pump ever more violence into us is because

In his report, Centerwall explains why homicide rates doubled in those countries and why the increase occurred when it did:

Given that homicide is primarily an adult activity, if television exerts its behavior-modifying effects primarily on children, the initial "television generation" would have had to age 10 to 15 years before they would have been old enough to affect the homicide rate. If this were so, it would be expected that, as the initial television generation grew up, rates of serious violence would first begin to rise among children, then several years later it would begin to rise among adolescents, then still later among young adults, and so on. And that is what is observed.

How much of the rise in homicide rates was a result of television? Centerwall explained: "To say that childhood exposure to television and television violence is a predisposing factor behind half of violent acts is not to discount the importance of other factors. Manifestly, every violent act is the result of an array of forces coming together—poverty, crime, alcohol and drug abuse, stress—of which childhood exposure to television is just one." He went on to suggest, however, that the evidence indicates that, if television had never been invented, there would be far less violent crime in the United States.

Some scientists dispute Centerwall's conclusion. Franklin Zimring and Gordon Hawkins of the University of California, Berkeley tested Centerwall's theory in four other Western countries: France, Germany, Italy, and Japan. They found that the homicide rate in those countries either stayed the same or declined as exposure to television increased. It is also worth noting that the homicide rate in the United States and Canada leveled off in 1975 and then declined, despite its residents' continuing and increasing exposure to television.

Sources: Brandon S. Centerwall, "Special Communication: Television and Violence: The Scale of the Problem and Where to Go from Here," *Journal of the American Medical Association*, vol. 267, no. 22 (June 10, 1992); Richard Rhodes, "The Media Violence Myth." *Rolling Stone*, November 23, 2000.

we've built up a tolerance. In order to get the same high, we need ever-higher levels. . . . The television industry has gained its market share through an addictive and toxic ingredient."[9] Video games may be particularly addictive because young players want to play for long periods of time to improve their scores and advance to higher levels.

QUOTABLE

Dr. Donald Cook, president of the American Academy of Pediatrics

In 2000, Donald Cook testified before a U.S. Senate committee on the effects of violent entertainment:

> Since the 1950s, more than 3,500 research studies in the United States and around the world using many investigative methods have examined whether there is an association between exposure to media violence and subsequent violent behavior. All but 18 have shown a positive correlation between media exposure and violent behavior. Some findings:
>
> • Epidemiologists studying a broad array of factors associated with violence, including poverty, racial discrimination, substance abuse, inadequate schools, joblessness, and family dissolution, found that exposure to violent media was a factor in half of the 10,000 homicides committed in the United States the previous year.
>
> • Numerous studies indicate that a preference for heavy metal music may be a significant marker for alienation, substance abuse, psychiatric disorders, suicide risk, sex-role stereotyping, or risk-taking behaviors during adolescence.
>
> • Research to date indicates that interactive media have an even more potent and lasting effect on violent behavior than passive media forms like television and movies. Several studies have shown that, after playing violent video games, children and adolescents become desensitized to violence, have increased levels of aggressive thoughts and behavior, and act hostile toward others.

All types of new media are especially dangerous.

The dividing line between traditional broadcast media and newer media has become blurred. Cable and satellite television, which are not governed by the FCC's Broadcast Decency Rule, make it possible for violent adult-rated films to be viewed by

- Studies designed to test the theory that experiencing media violence leads to a catharsis, a reduction in actual aggression due to the vicarious release of hostility, actually found increased overt aggression because of lowered inhibitions after experiencing media violence.

- Meta-analysis, a process by which the results from many different research studies are analyzed as a whole, shows that the strength of the correlation between exposure to media violence and aggressive behavior is larger than that of condom non-use and sexually transmitted HIV, lead exposure and lower IQ, passive tobacco smoke and lung cancer or calcium intake and bone mass, relationships which pediatricians accept as fact and on which we routinely base preventive medicine.

Children learn the ways of the world by observing and imitating—they cannot help but be influenced by media. Exposure to media violence, particularly violence perpetrated by dramatic heroes or, in the case of video games, the children themselves, results in an increased acceptance of violence as an appropriate means of conflict resolution. . . . Perhaps the most insidious and potent effect of media violence is that it desensitizes viewers to "real life" violence and to the harm caused its victims. . . .

Entertainment violence is not the sole factor contributing to youth aggression, antisocial attitudes, and violence. Family breakdown, peer influences, the availability of weapons, and numerous other factors may all play a part. But entertainment violence does contribute.

Source: Testimony of Donald E. Cook, M.D., president of the American Academy of Pediatrics, before the U.S. Senate Commerce Committee, September 13, 2000. http://www.aap.org/advocacy/releases/mediaviolencetestimony.pdf.

minors at home. In addition, some types of media reinforce one another. For example, music videos repeat the violent song lyrics the viewer heard elsewhere and often glorify violent characters. At the same time, the Internet makes it much easier to download entertainment, including violent video games that underage customers cannot legally rent from stores.

In recent years, much of the debate over new media has centered on violent video games. Using the same approach taken with respect to television, scientists have found a link between playing violent games and acting violently. Craig A. Anderson, a well-known researcher on effects of video games, and his colleague Brad J. Bushman, who analyzed 35 studies of these games, concluded that playing them increases aggression in males and females, in children and adults, and in experimental and non-experimental settings. In 2001, the American Academy of Pediatrics (AAP) concluded that playing violent games accounted for a 13 to 22 percent increase in teenagers' violent behavior—a risk factor equivalent to smoking, which accounts for a 14 percent increase in lung cancer.

The AAP explains how video games can make players more violent:

> Active participation increases effective learning. Video games are an ideal environment in which to learn violence. They place the player in the role of the aggressor and reward him or her for successful violent behavior. Rather than observing part of a violent interaction, video games allow the player to rehearse an entire behavioral script, from provocation, to choosing to respond violently, to resolution of the conflict.[10]

Some insist that violent games are capable of teaching players to kill. Authorities and psychologists have, in fact, attributed violent video games to the successful marksmanship of Michael Carneal, the West Paducah high school shooter, and John Lee Malvo, the teenage "Beltway sniper."

Some believe that video games of the future could be even more dangerous. Eugene Provenzo, a professor at the University of Miami, said:

> I've been trying hard to make people realize we're going into a very different culture as a result of the introduction of new technologies. . . . Video games are extremely powerful teaching machines, and we're still at a primitive level. We're on a trajectory toward increasing realism, or hyperreality, that makes people start thinking they can shoot someone and it doesn't hurt, that they can recover.[11]

Summary

Violent entertainment poses a greater threat to society than ever before. Young people—often unsupervised by their parents—are exposed to hours of entertainment every day. Violent entertainment is harmful to teenagers and especially children, whose developing minds cannot distinguish reality from fantasy. Young people imitate the violence they see, become desensitized to it, and accept it as a fact of life. The effects of violent entertainment increase with exposure, as is the case with cigarettes. As a result, the medical community considers violent entertainment a public health problem on a par with smoking. Many fear that new media, especially violent video games because of their interactive nature, have even greater potential to cause real-world violence.

The Dangers of Violent Entertainment Are Exaggerated

When laws restricting speech are challenged, judges require the government to offer strong evidence to support such restrictions. In cases involving violent entertainment, the courts have been skeptical of studies suggesting a link to real-world violence. In the 2009 case of *Video Software Dealers Association v. Schwarzenegger*, a federal appeals court assessed the scientific evidence linking violent video games to real-world violence:

> Nearly all of the research is based on correlation, not evidence of causation, and most of the studies suffer from significant, admitted flaws in methodology as they relate to the State's claimed interest. None of the research establishes or suggests a causal link between minors playing violent video games and actual psychological or neurological harm, and inferences to that

effect would not be reasonable. In fact, some of the studies caution against inferring causation.[1]

Studies linking violent entertainment to real-world violence are flawed.

Supporters of regulation cite studies showing a link between violent entertainment and real-life acts of violence. Some researchers, however, argue that those studies fail to prove that violent entertainment *causes* young people to commit violent acts. Jonathan Freedman, a professor of psychology at the University of Toronto, explains that just because two events are correlated—that is, associated with one another—one is not necessarily the cause of the other. He cites an example: Boys watch more football on television than girls and play more football than girls; however, no one argues that television is what makes boys more interested in football.

After a careful review, Freedman concluded that studies fail to prove that exposure to violent entertainment makes people more aggressive. He examined laboratory experiments, field experiments, and longitudinal studies and found flaws with each method. Freedman also concluded that field experiments, which he considered a more reliable test of whether violent entertainment caused real-world violence, did not prove the cause-and-effect hypothesis. Freedman offers an alternative explanation: Personality characteristics that make children more aggressive probably account for their preference for violent entertainment.

Some, like Professor Michael Males at the University of California, Santa Cruz, argue that laboratory conditions are so different from the real world that they have little value. A report by the Federal Communications Commission (FCC) sums up his criticisms:

> [Males] states that researchers have used vastly different examples of violent content in the cartoons, film clips,

or games that they study. He concludes that generalizations about all violence from these differing examples are not trustworthy and fail to account for the many different contexts in which works of art or entertainment present violence. . . . [H]e states that experimenters have not always made their nonviolent video clips equivalent to their violent ones with respect to other variables, such as general level of interest among children. . . . [H]e states that aggressive attitudes or "cognition" are not the same as aggressive behavior. Males asserts that proxies for aggression in lab experiments range from dubious (e.g., making noise blasts; hitting "Bobo dolls"; "killing" characters in a video game) to ludicrous (e.g., popping balloons). Finally, he states that aggressive play, whether in a lab or in the real world, is far different from real aggression intended to hurt another person.[2]

Critics exaggerate the impact of violent entertainment.

An oft-repeated assertion is that more than 3,500 research studies have examined the association between violence in the media and violent behavior, and all but 18 of those studies have shown a positive relationship. To begin with, the number of studies is likely exaggerated. Some researchers who have looked at the research into violent entertainment found fewer than 100 studies that focused specifically on whether television violence causes real-life aggression. Furthermore, the basis for that assertion is debatable. Researchers Lawrence Kutner and Cheryl K. Olson traced it back to an article published in 1998 by the United Nations, which failed to identify a source for the assertion.

Pro-regulation researchers have often been accused of bias. The Free Expression Policy Project, which opposes regulation, says: "In some cases, experimenters have manipulated disappointing results until they came up with at least one positive finding; then proclaimed that the experiment supported their hypothesis that media violence causes aggression."[3] Some also contend that studies that fail to blame violent entertainment are less likely to get published. Journalist Richard Rhodes adds that studies that find no link to real-world violence are not well known because they dispute the conventional wisdom about violent entertainment. Even the government has been accused of being less than impartial. Ronald Rotunda, a law professor at the University of Illinois, cites a 2000 Federal Trade Commission (FTC) investigation of the entertainment industry. According to Rotunda, the FTC set out to find a link between media violence and violent behavior but failed to do so. The agency buried that finding in an appendix to its report and focused instead on the *marketing* of violent entertainment to young audiences.

Finally, well-known studies of violent entertainment are less conclusive than advocates of regulation claim. For example, a 1972 report by the U.S. surgeon general found that the effect of television was small compared with many other possible causes; a 1982 study by the National Institute of Mental Health conceded that not all children who watched violent television became aggressive; and a 2001 report by the surgeon general observed that violent entertainment was more closely linked to aggressiveness than actual violence. The FTC report mentioned by Professor Rotunda expressed skepticism as to whether violent entertainment caused actual violence:

> Regarding *causation*, however, the studies appear to be less conclusive. Most researchers and investigators agree that exposure to media violence alone does not cause a child to commit a violent act, and that it is not the sole, or even necessarily the most important, factor contributing to youth aggression, antisocial attitudes, and violence.[4]

Real-world experience contradicts researchers' findings.

Contrary to the claims of those who urge regulation, there is evidence that crime rates are not related to the availability of violent entertainment. During the 1990s, when efforts to restrict violent video games began, advocates blamed them for the rising rate of juvenile crime in the United States. Soon afterward,

Protecting Young Internet Users from Harmful Material

In 1996, Congress passed the Communications Decency Act (CDA).* Subsection (a) made it illegal to knowingly transmit obscene or indecent material to a person younger than 18, and subsection (d) outlawed the knowing display of material that "depicts or describes, in terms patently offensive as measured by contemporary community standards, sexual or excretory activities or organs" to a person younger than 18. Violating the CDA was a federal crime.

A legal challenge to the CDA quickly reached the U.S. Supreme Court, which, in *Reno v. American Civil Liberties Union*, 521 U.S. 344 (1997), found both provisions of the CDA unconstitutional. The vote was seven to two. Justice John Paul Stevens wrote the Court's opinion. He rejected the government's contention that the Internet, like broadcast media, had a lower level of First Amendment protection. He concluded that the Internet was not as invasive as broadcast television and radio, nor did it have the same history of regulation. Justice Stevens also concluded that the CDA was too vague: it did not define "indecent" or "patently offensive," or explain how those terms related to one another. Furthermore, the law not only "chilled" speech by forcing content providers to guess where the legal line was, but it also forced a person facing charges to prove in court that he or she took steps to exclude underage users. In addition, Justice Stevens concluded that the government had not shown why certain measures would protect young users from harmful content. Those measures included requiring posters to "tag" adult-only content, limiting the CDA to commercial Web sites, and exempting content with serious social value.

however, crime by young people fell sharply. From 1994 to 2001, arrests for murder, rape, robbery, and aggravated assaults fell 44 percent, resulting in the lowest juvenile arrest rate for violent crimes since 1993. Murder arrests, which had reached a high of 3,800 in 1983, fell to 1,400 by 2001. Furthermore, evidence suggests that the rise in juvenile crime during the 1980s and 1990s was due in large part to the general increase in crime in inner

Congress responded to the *Reno* decision by passing the Child Online Protection Act (COPA),** a narrower law that applied only to those who posted, for "commercial purposes," content defined as "harmful to minors"—a definition based on the Supreme Court's standard of obscenity. COPA also applied only to the World Wide Web and excluded regions of cyberspace such as chat rooms. Nevertheless, COPA was challenged in court. The legal dispute ended in February 2009, when the Supreme Court let stand an appeals court decision*** that found the law unconstitutional. The lower courts had expressed concern over COPA's overly broad language, believing its "harmful to minors" standard could apply to material with social value, and its blanket definition of "minors" made no allowances for 16- and 17-year-olds. In addition, the lower courts were troubled by COPA's "community standards" test, under which the most conservative communities might exercise veto power over the rest of the country. The lower courts also indicated that technology that blocked young peoples' access to pornography might be a better, and less restrictive, approach than a law carrying criminal penalties. Finally, the lower courts recognized both the difficulty of verifying ages online and the chilling effect of requiring a Web site operator to prove that he or she took steps to deny access to those younger than 18.

The downfall of CDA and COPA resulted from the Supreme Court's applying a "strict-scrutiny" standard to laws restricting speech. Legal experts believe that this test makes it very difficult for lawmakers to write a "harmful to minors" statute that can stand up in court, especially if the material in question is something other than pornography.

* 47 U.S.C. §223.
** 47 U.S.C. §231.
*** *American Civil Liberties Union v. Mukasey*, 534 F.3d 181 (3d Cir. 2008).

cities, *not* the fact that young inner-city residents watched more violent entertainment than the population as a whole.

Author Gerard Jones says that America's experience with television in the 1970s contradicts the claim that televised violence contributes to real violence. During that decade, advocacy groups such as Action for Children's Television pressured the networks to cut down on violence. Jones explains what happened during those years:

> Crime rates increased. Our national anxiety about violence, as measured by opinion polls, worsened. The kids who spent their formative years in that pop-cultural milieu became the teenagers of the mid-1980s, when crime rates rose again. The kids who spent their formative years in the 1980s, on the other hand, when action-packed movies, TV shows, video games, and combat toys seemed to be taking over kid culture, became the teenagers of the late 1990s, when those rates plummeted.[5]

Furthermore, millions of Americans watch violent content and play violent video games, yet most are never arrested for a violent crime. This also applies internationally. Many young Asians, for example, also play violent video games, yet we rarely hear about Columbine-type attacks in their countries.

Finally, young people do not necessarily imitate what they see in the media. Benjamin Radford, the managing editor of *Skeptical Inquirer* magazine, observes:

> Daily teen life involves [exposure to] some profanity, adult themes, and violent entertainment. Has the sexual material resulted in an increase in teen sex? No; the National Center for Health Statistics reported last year that fewer teens are engaging in sexual activity than in the past, and the rate dropped significantly between

1995 and 2002. . . . Has the video violence resulted in an increase in violent crime? No; on Oct. 17, 2005, the FBI released figures showing that the U.S. violent crime rate declined again last year. In fact, violent crime has dropped significantly over the past twenty years—just as video games have become more violent.[6]

Author Marjorie Heins adds that young people react differently to the same entertainment: Some might imitate what they see, while others may experience catharsis.

Other factors are responsible for crime.

Much of the evidence linking game playing to violent behavior is anecdotal—that is, based on individual stories, not scientific research or data. It also turns out that important details of these stories are inaccurate. After the Columbine shootings, critics blamed violent video games for inciting Dylan Klebold and Eric Harris to carry out the massacre. An FBI investigation of the shootings, however, disputed such a link, instead blaming the shooters' mental problems: Klebold suffered from depression, and Harris was a sociopath. Likewise, video games were blamed for Seung-Hui Cho's gunning down of 32 people at Virginia Tech University in 2007. It was later found that Cho, suffering from serious mental problems, had been referred to court-ordered outpatient treatment and did not seem to play video games.

Because many factors go into making a person violent, it is difficult to demonstrate what factors, added together, might produce a sociopath. In fact, the federal government tried to develop a "shooter profile" to help prevent future mass shootings but could not do so because shooter events were so rare and so many factors combined to produce them. Other experts have come to similar conclusions. According to Maggie Cutler:

The American Psychological Association's Commission on Violence and Youth (1994) mentions violent media as only one among many factors in juvenile violence. It stresses that inborn temperament, early parental abuse or neglect, poverty, cognitive impairment, plus a deficiency of corrective influences or role models in various combinations will put a child at greater risk for violence, both as perpetrator and as victim.[7]

Flaws in Studies Linking Violent Entertainment and Real-World Violence

Lawrence Kutner and Cheryl K. Olson, faculty members at Harvard Medical School, are the authors of *Grand Theft Childhood*, a book that summarizes the results of their study of the effects of playing violent video games and challenges the claim that playing such games inspires real-life violence.

Kutner and Olson explain: "To understand the claims made by researchers, it's useful to know how scientists approach a complex problem like the causes of violence. Scientific research is like solving a jigsaw puzzle in which you don't know if you have all the pieces; the pieces that you do have can fit together in many different ways and you're not sure what the finished picture will look like."

The authors argue that studies can be misleading for a number of reasons:

- The study population is unrepresentative. For example, college students who are paid to play games are different from teenagers who play for entertainment.

- Research subjects do not play games the same way they are played in real life. For example, subjects play for short periods of time, while actual players may play for hours.

- Not all video game play exposes the player to the same amount of violence. That is true even of multiple players who play the same game.

- Aggression is not the same as violence. People who act aggressively do not necessarily commit acts of violence. Furthermore, aggression is hard to measure. In fact, since there is no accepted measure of aggression, experts have devised a number of surrogate measures for it.

- Even when studies find a statistically significant increase in aggressiveness—in other words, the measured difference was probably not the

A year earlier, another APA report, *Violence & Youth*, concluded that the greatest predictor of future violent behavior was a previous history of violence. In fact, Dr. Laurence Steinberg, a leading expert on child development, argues that the various forms of media probably rank at the bottom of the list of factors that cause a child to become violent.

result of chance—the increase might be too small to represent a major contribution to violent behavior.

- Studies fail to distinguish among populations of game players. In particular, some young players are more likely than others to act violently.

- Some researchers are biased in favor of finding a link between game-playing and violence. They refuse to submit for publication those studies that fail to produce the results they wanted or expected.

Kutner and Olson also contend that some advocacy groups use faulty logic in blaming video games for violent behavior. One common error is mistaking correlation and causation. Studies may show that young people who play violent games are more likely to commit acts of violence, but that does not necessarily prove that game playing *causes* violence. Kutner and Olson explain: "[I]t's likely that children who are already more aggressive than their peers prefer and seek out violent media programs and games. It's possible that time spent with a violent game or movie could help shape or trigger aggressive impulses in aggressive children. Perhaps a high level of violent media consumption could be a marker for existing aggression." Another error is *post hoc ergo propter hoc*, which means wrongly concluding that if event A happened before event B, then event A caused event B. They cite the case of Shawn Woolley, a suicide victim who was a heavy player of the video game *EverQuest*. Shawn's mother blamed the game for his death, but Kutner and Olson point out that Shawn had a history of mental illness: "It's much more likely that [Shawn's] obsessive video game playing was a reflection of his other, more profound problems—a way he tried unsuccessfully to handle the intense emotions and stress he was feeling—and not the root cause of his suicide."

Source: Lawrence Kutner and Cheryl K. Olson, *Grand Theft Childhood: The Surprising Truth About Violent Video Games and What Parents Can Do.* New York: Simon & Schuster, 2008.

WILLIAM WALLACE.

Scottish hero Sir William Wallace led a revolt against the British crown during the Wars of Scottish Independence. In 1305, Wallace was brutally and publicly executed. Today, such violent executions are considered unacceptable, and even the death penalty itself is outlawed in most nations.

Legal challenges to video game regulations have exposed flaws in studies that link games to real-world violence. Dr. Craig A. Anderson, the author of numerous studies suggesting such a link, has often testified on behalf of the government. In *Entertainment Software Association v. Blagojevich* (2005), the judge observed that Anderson's studies failed to eliminate the most obvious alternative explanation—namely, that aggressive individuals may themselves be attracted to violent video games. Causation is very important in the law. In *James v. Meow Media, Inc.* (2002), a federal appeals court absolved entertainment companies of liability for the West Paducah school shooting. Judge Danny Boggs's opinion explained why the shooter's exposure to violent entertainment was not the legal cause of the students' deaths:

> It appears simply impossible to predict that these games, movie, and Internet sites (alone, or in what combinations) would incite a young person to violence. . . . We find that it is simply too far a leap from shooting characters on a video screen (an activity undertaken by millions) to shooting people in a classroom (an activity undertaken by a handful, at most) for Carneal's actions to have been reasonably foreseeable to the manufacturers of the media that Carneal played and viewed.[8]

Furthermore, blaming violent entertainment for violent crime is contrary to our society's notions of personal responsibility. It also teaches children the wrong lesson: If they misbehave, they might say that a television show, film, or video game "made them do it."

Violent entertainment is replacing real-world violence.

In 1305, Scottish rebel leader William Wallace was publicly and very gruesomely executed outside London. Nearly 700 years later, a version of that execution—with much of the violence implied and not seen—was shown in the film *Braveheart.*

Some, like journalist Richard Rhodes, consider the depiction of Wallace's execution in *Braveheart* a sign of social progress:

> The whole thrust of socialization across the past thousand years in Western culture has been toward reducing private violence in order to foster more effective social interaction in an increasingly complex and interdependent society. . . . As people moved away from malevolence toward civility, the pleasure of doing violence was gradually displaced by the pleasure of seeing violence done—such as watching public executions and attending cockfights, bullfights, and bare-knuckle boxing matches.[9]

Rhodes adds that humans are becoming less tolerant of real-world cruelty. Public executions have been done away with in most of the world (in fact, many Western countries have abolished the death penalty altogether), and violent sports such as bullfighting, fox-hunting, and even boxing have become less acceptable.

Harold Schechter, a professor at Queens College in New York, argues that, as civilization advances, it replaces real-world violence with violent entertainment. One good example is the Grand Guignol, a theater company that operated in Paris from the 1890s until 1962. It specialized in gruesome melodramas, which literally sickened some members of the audience. Even though the plays at the Grand Guignol appealed to humans' age-old hunger to watch violence and brutality, Schechter points out that "they can be seen in a far more positive light—as a sign of how much progress we've made in devising clever ways to satisfy those dark primal urges. After all, even the most grisly productions in the Grand Guignol's repertoire were only make-believe. No one really got hurt."[10] Another was the Torture Chamber at the 1933 World's Fair in Chicago, which graphically depicted acts of barbarity, complete with lifelike models and recorded screams. Schechter observes:

> [T]he 1933 World's Fair Torture Chamber really was a sign of our progress as a civilization, since it showed that, in the span of only a few centuries—the blink of an eye in evolutionary terms—the citizens of Western society had renounced real torture as a form of entertainment and accepted counterfeit cruelty in its place: mechanical tricks performed with gears, cams, and levers and perpetrated on motorized dummies.[11]

Schechter suggests that we have made further progress since 1933, noting that a torture exhibition purely for entertainment would likely be unacceptable today.

Summary

Studies showing a link between exposure to violent entertainment and real violence are flawed because they do not reflect real-life conditions, confuse aggressive behavior with actual violence, and fail to recognize that violent people gravitate to violent entertainment. Some researchers exaggerate the role violent entertainment plays in causing actual violence and are biased in favor of blaming entertainment for such violence. Real-world experience contradicts studies that link entertainment to violence. Crime, especially by young people, has fallen in recent years, even though entertainment is as violent as ever. Millions of Americans enjoy such entertainment without committing any criminal acts. Some even believe that society is civilizing itself by replacing real-world violence with violent entertainment.

The Entertainment Industry Has Acted Irresponsibly

In 2003, Mary Lou Dickerson, a Washington state representative, expressed her concern about the effects of violent video games:

> We've been seeing a whole rash of shootings throughout this country and in Europe that relate back to kids who obsessively play violent video games. The kids involved as shooters in Columbine were obsessively playing violent video games. We know after the Beltway sniper incident where the seventeen-year-old [Lee Malvo] was a fairly good shot, but [John Allen] Muhammad, the police tell us, got him to practice on an ultraviolent video game in sniper mode to break down his hesitancy to kill.[1]

The link between violent games and the "Beltway sniper" killings suggests that violent entertainment is a dangerous product that is marketed irresponsibly to young people. (In the Beltway sniper attacks, Muhammad and Malvo killed 10 people in the Washington, D.C., area over a three-week period in October 2002.)

Entertainment has become coarser.

When modern ratings first appeared in 1968, it was unusual for a film to earn an "X" rating, the equivalent of today's "NC-17" rating. Nowadays, NC-17 films are shown on cable television, where even small children can watch them. Furthermore, today's NC-17 films are more violent than those of the past. Author Gregg Easterbrook points out that, at first, adult ratings were given to films that depicted sexual situations or expressed controversial political views, rather than those that showed graphic violence. For example, the 1971 film *A Clockwork Orange* was rated X even though it depicted only one killing—which was heard but not shown on the screen. The trend toward greater violence is not limited to film. A 2007 study by the Parents Television Council found that violence on television between 8 and 10 P.M. had increased substantially in recent years. Others found that scenes of sexual violence have become increasingly common on prime-time television. All too often these scenes provide a young viewer's first exposure to a sexual situation.

Other forms of entertainment have grown coarser as well. Few of the earliest video games were violent. Nolan Bushnell, the creator of Atari, one of the early game makers, had a policy against depicting violence against people. By contrast, today's video games not only depict such violence, but they also allow the player to become the perpetrator of it. Song lyrics have become more violent and also contain more foul and derogatory language and references to sexual activity and drug use than those of a generation ago. Music videos often depict violence and weapons. Some critics wonder why, in a society plagued by bad parenting and easy access to weaponry, the entertainment industry insists on making violence even more prevalent.

Competition for audiences has resulted in a "race to the bottom" within the entertainment industry. Newton Minow, the former chairman of the Federal Communications Commission (FCC), said:

> [B]roadcasters convinced themselves that the secret to "competition" lay not in distinguishing their programming from what was available on cable but in copying it. The competition, such as it was, was to reclaim the well-off younger viewers whom advertisers wanted to reach and who had migrated in significant numbers to cable. To lure them back, broadcasters began to experiment with programs on topics and issues once considered off-limits—much of the material, like cable programming, with strong sexual or violent content.[2]

Violent entertainment encourages antisocial behavior.

In 2000, Dr. Donald Cook, the president of the American Academy of Pediatrics, explained to a U.S. Senate committee:

> The more realistic, comic, or enjoyable the media violence, the greater the desensitization—video games that reward killing with points and higher levels of play are using better graphics capabilities to increase the gore, showing spraying blood and mangled body parts, or to personalize games with digital images such as recognizable faces on victims.[3]

Violent entertainment also encourages disrespect of others, especially women and members of minority groups. A resolution by the American Psychological Association (APA) on video game violence cited studies that linked sexualized violence in the media to increased violence against women and rape. Hip-hop music has been condemned as demeaning to women, gay men, and lesbians. Worse yet, groups with extreme political views are using violent entertainment to spread hate speech against members of minority groups. Extremist groups also use entertainment to recruit young people, many of whom are receptive to racist views because they have had little contact with people of other races.

Such entertainment also perpetuates stereotypes. During the 1970s, a genre of films called "blaxploitation" made its appearance. These films featured urban settings and African-American actors and had soundtracks of funk and soul music. Many critics believed that these films, although written and produced largely by African Americans, stereotyped black men as pimps and drug dealers. The same is true of today's hip-hop music. Professor Tricia Rose of Brown University explains: "The depths of the commercial success associated with violent, gang, and street culture as 'authentic' hip-hop has given violent black masculinity a seal of approval, thus encouraging these behaviors among the kids who are most at risk, and who 'need' to embrace this model if manhood is to survive."[4] Rose adds that hip-hop songs depict stereotypes about African Americans to an audience that is often white and suburban.

Violent entertainment also encourages a variety of other antisocial behavior, just as other entertainment portrays smoking, drinking, recreational drug use, and sexual promiscuity in a favorable light and thus encourages members of the audience—many of whom are still in their teens—to engage in that behavior. An example of this antisocial behavior can be seen in a video game called *Bully*, in which the player can hurt other students in school. A screen shot from the game depicts one student kicking a classmate while another looks on.

Entertainment companies market violent content to underage audiences.

The easing of government regulations on media companies has resulted in most of the entertainment industry being owned by a few powerful companies. Executives of these companies are paid to attract the largest possible audience and tend to be motivated

FROM THE BENCH

Chaplinsky v. New Hampshire, 315 U.S. 568 (1942) and Brandenburg v. Ohio, 395 U.S. 444 (1969)

In *Chaplinsky v. New Hampshire*, the U.S. Supreme Court declared that "fighting words" are one category of speech not protected by the First Amendment. The case began when Walter Chaplinsky, a member of the Jehovah's Witnesses, was arrested after he called one individual "a G** damned racketeer" and another "a damned Fascist" while distributing pamphlets outside City Hall in Rochester, New Hampshire. The law under which Chaplinsky was arrested made it illegal to "address an offensive, derisive, or annoying word" at anyone or call a person by an "offensive or derisive name" in a public place.

After the trial court convicted him, Chaplinsky appealed. He contended that the First Amendment protected his remarks. His appeal went to the U.S. Supreme Court, which unanimously affirmed his conviction. Regarding Chaplinsky's freedom of speech, Justice Frank Murphy wrote in the Court's opinion:

> There are certain well-defined and narrowly limited classes of speech, the prevention and punishment of which has never been thought to raise any Constitutional problem. These include the lewd and obscene, the profane, the libelous, and the insulting or "fighting" words—those which by their very utterance inflict injury or tend to incite an immediate breach of the peace. It has been well observed that such utterances are no essential part of any exposition of ideas, and are of such slight social value as a step to truth that any benefit that may be derived from them is clearly outweighed by the social interest in order and morality.

Justice Murphy concluded that "offensive" meant language a person of common intelligence would consider "fighting words," which were likely to provoke that person into retaliating.

more by profits than by ethical standards. Some critics of violent entertainment argue that broadcasting violent programs to children is as callous as distributing dangerous toys, building homes with lead-based paint, or selling guns to minors. They also reject the media companies' argument that consumers have "veto power" over offensive entertainment because they can refuse

A generation later, the Supreme Court revisited the issue of incitement to violence in *Brandenburg v. Ohio*. While Charles Brandenburg, a leader of the Ku Klux Klan, spoke at a Klan rally in the Cincinnati area, he said, among other things, "[I]f our president, our Congress, our Supreme Court, continues to suppress the white, Caucasian race, it's possible that there might have to be some revengeance [sic] taken." He also said, "Send the Jews back to Israel" and "Bury the n*****s."

Brandenburg was charged with violating Ohio's criminal syndicalism law, which forbade "advocat[ing] . . . the duty, necessity, or propriety of crime, sabotage, violence, or unlawful methods of terrorism as a means of accomplishing industrial or political reform." Toward the end of World War I, a number of states had passed such laws to control radical groups that sometimes engaged in violent protest. The trial court found Brandenburg guilty and sentenced him to one to ten years in prison and a $1,000 fine. His appeal eventually reached the U.S. Supreme Court, which unanimously reversed his conviction.

The Court's opinion was brief and *per curiam*, meaning that it was not attributed to any particular justice. The justices noted that, in the first half of the twentieth century, the Court affirmed convictions under criminal syndicalism laws but later reversed itself and held that the First Amendment barred the government from prosecuting a person for advocacy unless that advocacy was "directed to inciting or producing imminent lawless action and is likely to incite or produce such action." They concluded that Ohio's criminal syndicalism statute "by its words and as applied, purports to punish mere advocacy and to forbid, on pain of criminal punishment, assembly with others merely to advocate the described type of action" and therefore, "falls within the condemnation of the First and Fourteenth Amendments."

to watch it. Professor Rose responds: "[T]his suggestion would make it seem normal for the mass media industry to retain the power to decide what gets presented, and our only power is to turn it off. Yes, we should turn it off when we want to. But that's simply not enough. What gets presented creates audience desire as much as it reflects it."[5]

In 2000, the Federal Trade Commission (FTC) issued a report that criticized the entertainment industry's marketing practices:

> [C]ompanies . . . routinely target children under 17 as the audience for movies, music, and games that their own rating or labeling systems say are inappropriate for children or warrant parental caution due to their violent content. Moreover, children under 17 frequently are able to buy tickets to R-rated movies without being accompanied by an adult and can easily purchase music recordings and electronic games that have a parental advisory label or are restricted to an older audience.[6]

The FTC cited marketing plans that explicitly targeted those younger than 18 for some adult-rated material. Other adult-rated entertainment, while not specifically marketed to underage audiences, was advertised in media with a significant youth audience. The FTC found that entertainment companies had even recruited children as young as 10 to take part in focus groups for adult-rated films.

Such marketing practices by entertainment companies are comparable to those once used to sell cigarettes to young people. In the 1980s, a cartoon character named Joe Camel appeared in advertisements for Camel cigarettes. Camel's share of the under-18 market—people too young to buy cigarettes legally—rose sharply. Among small children, Joe Camel was more recognizable than Ronald McDonald. Even though multiple studies have shown that violent entertainment, like tobacco, is toxic to minors, entertainment companies systematically market it to young customers. A recent article by Nicholas L. Carnagey, Craig A. Anderson, and Brad J. Bushman explains:

> Children receive high doses of media violence. It initially is packaged in ways that are not too threatening, with cute cartoon-like characters, a total absence of blood and gore, and other features that make the overall experience a pleasant one, arousing positive emotional reactions that are incongruent with normal negative reactions to violence. Older children consume increasingly threatening and realistic violence, but the increases are gradual and always in a way that is fun.[7]

Industry self-regulation is weak.

Entertainment has become more violent in part because industry ratings have become more lenient. Films with a considerable amount of graphic violence are given a rating of "R" or even "PG-13." In recent years, the problem has been compounded by the appearance of unrated versions of films, which often contain material that was deleted before a film's release in order to earn a less-restrictive rating. Some critics of the current rating system believe that it is at least as easy for young people to obtain the more-graphic unrated version as the adult-rated version.

Today's ratings have gotten out of step with the views of many parents—the very group the ratings were intended to help. According to the American Academy of Pediatrics (AAP), parents found that as much as 50 percent of all television shows rated "TV-14" were inappropriate for their teenage children. It is not surprising that broadcasters underrate their programs. To begin with, there is an economic incentive to do so: A more restrictive rating diminishes the audience and thus reduces advertising revenue. Another reason is the makeup of rating boards. Advocates

(continues on page 65)

Entertainment Industry Ratings Systems

Motion Pictures

The Motion Picture Association of America (MPAA) introduced the current age-based system of motion picture ratings in 1968:

- "G" means rated "general audiences." The MPAA ratings board found nothing that would offend parents whose younger children watch the film.

- "PG" means "parental guidance suggested." The film may contain mature themes, some profanity, or some depictions of violence or brief nudity.

- "PG-13" means "parents strongly cautioned" because some material may be inappropriate for those younger than 13. The film may contain violence, nudity, sensuality, language, or adult activities; however, that content is not intense enough to earn an "R" rating. Drug use and certain profanity require at least a PG-13 rating.

- "R" means "restricted," in which no one younger than 17 may be admitted without a parent. The film may contain, for example, adult themes or activity, hard language, intense or persistent violence, sexually oriented nudity, or drug abuse.

- "NC-17" means "no one 17 and under admitted." An NC-17 film carries that rating because of violence, sex, aberrational behavior, drug abuse, or some other element that most parents would consider too strong for their children to watch.

Although the MPAA system has been criticized as lacking in detail and being too lenient, it is the model for other industries' rating systems.

Music

Since 1985, the Recording Industry Association of America (RIAA) has overseen a "Parental Advisory Label" program that applies to recordings containing explicit lyrics.

Record companies, not the RIAA, decide whether a recording contains explicit lyrics. According to the RIAA, less than five percent of albums released by the major record companies fall into that category. The packaging for a record containing explicit lyrics must bear a non-removable black-and-white "parental advisory" label.

Many retailers refuse to sell albums with a parental-advisory label to customers younger than 18 or to handle labeled recordings altogether, and many retailers try to verify the age of would-be buyers.

Television

The TV Parental Guidelines began in 1997. Although technically voluntary, federal legislation that required the installation of a V-chip in television sets forced the broadcasting industry to develop the ratings, which are required on all programming except news and sports. Producers rate their own programs. Ratings appear in the upper left-hand corner of the television screen for the first 15 seconds of a program.

There are four ratings for an all-ages audience:

- "G" means "general audience." Most parents would find it suitable for all ages and may allow younger children to watch by themselves.

- "PG" means "parental guidance suggested." The program contains material that parents may find unsuitable for younger children. It may contain some suggestive dialogue ("D"), infrequent coarse language ("L"), some sexual situations ("S"), or moderate violence ("V").

- "14" means "parents strongly cautioned." The program contains material that many parents would find unsuitable for those younger than 14. It may contain intensely suggestive dialogue, strong coarse language, intense sexual situations, or intense violence.

- "MA" means "mature audience only." The program is intended to be watched by adults and therefore may be unsuitable for those younger than 17. It may contain indecent language; explicit sexual activity; or graphic violence.

In addition, three ratings apply only to children's programming:

- "Y" means "all children." The program is appropriate for children as young as age 2 and is not expected to frighten younger children.

- "Y7" means "directed to older children." Themes and elements in the program may include mild fantasy violence or comedic violence, or may frighten children younger than 7.

(continues)

(continued)

- "Y7 FV" means "fantasy violence." The fantasy violence may be more intense or more combative than other programs in the Y7 category.

Video Games

Established in 1994, the Entertainment Software Rating Board (ESRB) has a ratings system that consist of a symbol, which is age-based, along with "content descriptors," which identify those elements that provide the basis for the game's rating or may otherwise be of interest to parents.

The rating symbols are:

- "EC," which means "early childhood." The game may be suitable for children age 3 or older. There is no content that parents would find inappropriate.

- "E," which means "everyone." The game may be suitable for children age 6 or older. It may contain minimal cartoon, fantasy, or mild violence, or infrequent use of mild language.

- "E10+," which means "everyone 10 and older." It may contain cartoon, fantasy, or mild violence, mild language, or minimally suggestive themes.

- "T," which means "teen," or suitable for players age 13 or older. It may contain violence, suggestive themes, crude humor, minimal blood, simulated gambling, or infrequent use of strong language.

- "M," which means "mature," or suitable for players age 17 and older. It may contain intense violence, blood and gore, sexual content, or strong language.

- "AO," which means "adults only," or suitable only for those at least 18 years old. It may include prolonged scenes of intense violence or graphic sexual content and nudity.

- "RP," which means "rating pending."

The 30 content descriptors alert parents to violence; depictions of or references to alcohol or drug use, smoking, or gambling; coarse language; or sexual content or nudity.

(continued from page 61)
point out that most board members have ties to the industry and that parents and child advocates are underrepresented on these boards.

Existing rating systems are also confusing. A 2004 Kaiser Family Foundation survey of television ratings found:

> [O]nly 24 percent of parents of young children (two–six years old) could name any of the ratings that would apply to programming appropriate for children that age. Only 12 percent of parents knew that the rating FV ("fantasy violence") is related to violent content, while 8 percent thought it meant "family viewing." One in five (20 percent) parents said that they had never heard of the TV ratings system, an increase from 14 percent in 2000 and 2001. A more recent survey indicates that only 8 percent of respondents could correctly identify the categories.[8]

Adding to the confusion is that each medium has its own rating system. Dale Kunkel, a professor at the University of California, Santa Barbara, told a Senate committee:

> [A] media product that included extreme violence would be rated R if it were a movie, TV-MA if it were a TV show, M if it were a home video game, display a red sticker if it were an arcade video game, or have a "Parental Advisory" sticker if it were a music CD. This causes needless confusion for parents, and undercuts the utility of all rating systems.[9]

Nor has technology—most notably the V-chip that was offered as an alternative to regulation—protected young people from violent entertainment. In 2007, the FCC concluded that studies showed that the V-chip was of limited effectiveness in protecting children from violent television programs. The FCC also cited a survey conducted by the Kaiser Family Foundation that found that only 15 percent of parents used the V-chip, and another survey that blamed the low usage rate on parents'

The Federal Government Investigates Entertainment Marketing Practices

In June 1999, President Bill Clinton asked the Federal Trade Commission (FTC) to conduct a study of the marketing practices of the motion picture, recording, and video game industries. The FTC report, released in 2000, found:

Despite the variations in the three industries' systems, the outcome is consistent: Individual companies in each industry routinely market to children the very products that have the industries' own parental warnings or ratings with age restrictions due to their violent content. Indeed, for many of these products, the Commission found evidence of marketing and media plans that expressly target children under 17. In addition, the companies' marketing and media plans showed strategies to promote and advertise their products in the media outlets most likely to reach children under 17.

The FTC specifically found:

- With respect to motion pictures, 35 out of 44 films rated R for violence—or 80 percent—were targeted to movie-goers younger than 17. The marketing plans for 28 of those 35 films contained express statements that the target audience included under-17s. For example, one plan for a violent R-rated film stated, "Our goal was to find the elusive teen target audience and make sure everyone between the ages of 12–18 was exposed to the film." The marketing documents for seven other films did not expressly identify an under-17 target audience but were either similar to those that explicitly mentioned that audience or detailed actions consistent with targeting it, such as promoting the film in high schools or in publications where most readers were teenagers or younger.

- With respect to recorded music, the marketing plans for 15 out of 55—or 27 percent—of music recordings with a "parental advisory" label expressly identified teenagers as part of their target audience. Even though the

unawareness of the chip and the difficulty of programming it. Because so few parents use the V-chip, the Parents Television Council says that the broadcasting industry's effort to educate parents about the chip is a failure.

marketing documents for the other 40 records did not expressly mention the age of the target audience, they described the same methods of marketing as those plans that specifically targeted teenagers.

- With respect to video games, 83 of the 118—or 70 percent—of electronic games with a "Mature" rating for violence targeted players younger than 17. The marketing plans for 60 games expressly included under-17s as their target audience, and those for 23 other games contained plans to advertise in magazines or on television shows with a majority or substantial under-17 audience.

The FTC also concluded that most retailers made little effort to restrict underage access to entertainment with violent content. FTC-commissioned surveys found that just over half of movie theaters admitted patrons aged 13 to 16 to R-rated films, even when not accompanied by an adult, and that unaccompanied customers aged 13 to 16 were able to buy explicit-content recordings and M-rated electronic games 85 percent of the time.

The FTC said that "the mere publication of codes is not sufficient" and called on the entertainment industry to enhance its self-regulatory efforts. It specifically recommended that they do the following:

1. Establish or expand codes that prohibit target marketing to children and teenagers, and impose meaningful penalties on offenders.

2. Increase compliance at the retail level by checking identification or requiring parental permission before selling tickets to R-rated films, and by refusing to sell or rent recordings with a "Parental Advisory" label or video games with an M or AO rating to underage customers.

3. Increase parental understanding of the ratings and labels, including spelling out the reasons for giving a product an age-restricted rating.

Source: Federal Trade Commission. *Marketing Violent Entertainment to Children: A Review of Self-Regulation and Industry Practices in the Motion Picture, Music Recording & Electronic Game Industries.* Washington, D.C., 2000.

Parents need the government's help.

New technology, combined with the entertainment industry's marketing practices, has undermined parental authority. Professor Kevin W. Saunders argues:

> Not only should parents have the right to control the influences to which their children are exposed, it is a part of the job of parenting. But parents need help in discharging that responsibility. It may have been easy to make sure that children were exposed to the right influences in an earlier era. Children are now subjected to far more influences, from videos to cable television to video games to the Internet, than when the issues were simply what books to read or which of the television network broadcasts to watch.[10]

The FTC's finding of widespread noncompliance with the various rating systems suggests that a system of regulation without the force of law will not work. Nor has the FTC done enough to hold companies accountable for their marketing practices. In 2000, Charlie Condon, the attorney general of South Carolina, remarked: "When Hollywood, using its financial wealth and slick ads to excite, hypnotize and entice youngsters, subverts parental authority through deceptive and unfair practices, then we have the responsibility to enforce existing laws banning such practices."[11] Condon contended that the entertainment companies' marketing practices already met the definition of an "unfair trade practice" under existing laws.

Some advocates believe that state officials should file lawsuits against the entertainment industry, just as they did against the tobacco industry in the 1990s. The tobacco lawsuits resulted in a settlement agreement that, among other things, obligated the tobacco companies to end certain marketing practices that the states' attorneys general believed encouraged young people to smoke. Some members of the legal community even advocate

suing entertainment companies for putting a dangerous product on the market. Jack Thompson, a lawyer in Florida, sued
the companies that sold violent video games and other material to Michael Carneal, the West Paducah high school shooter.
Although a federal appeals court dismissed the lawsuit, observers point out that it took years for the courts to hold tobacco
companies legally responsible for the damage their products did
to smokers.

Summary

The amount and intensity of violent entertainment has increased
in recent years, and it is often shown at times when small children are in the audience. Competition has produced a "race to
the bottom," in which companies lower their standards to attract
bigger audiences. In addition to violence, entertainment encourages other antisocial behavior, including racism, bullying, and
substance abuse. Entertainment companies systematically market adult-rated content to teenagers and even preteens, despite
objections from parents and public officials. Many consider
industry self-regulation a failure because noncompliance is
widespread, ratings are too permissive and confusing to parents,
and technology such as the television V-chip has done little
to stop young viewers from watching violent programs. Many
advocates believe that government regulation is the only way to
improve the industry's behavior.

Critics Wrongly Blame Entertainment for Crime

O n Thanksgiving Day in 2001, 21-year-old Shawn Woolley fatally shot himself. His mother blamed the video game *EverQuest*, which Shawn had played obsessively for years, for his suicide. She had reason to blame *EverQuest*, which had a reputation among players for being addictive. Lawrence Kutner and Cheryl K. Olson, however, offer another explanation: Shawn had a history of mental problems, including schizoid personality disorder, an illness characterized by avoiding people and gravitating toward solitary activities such as playing video games. Kutner and Olson argue: "It's much more likely that [Shawn's] obsessive video game playing was a reflection of his other, more profound problems—a way he tried unsuccessfully to handle the intense emotions and stress he was feeling—and not the root cause of his suicide."[1] The rush to blame video games for Woolley's death is an example of how the entertainment industry is wrongly blamed for real-world violence.

Entertainment merely reflects real-world violence.

Human beings' elemental violent nature influences our choices in entertainment. Professor Harold Schechter reminds us that human beings have a violent history:

> Given humanity's innate endowment of aggression and cruelty—an instinctual inheritance from our archaic past—it's no surprise that we require outlets for our bloodthirsty tendencies. . . . After all, as a species we've been "civilized" for only a few millennia, compared to the many millions of years we existed as savage hominids who lived by hunting and slaughter.[2]

In his book *Savage Pastimes*, Schechter cites a long list of brutal exhibitions that entertained the public in years past. They included public executions, plays depicting the torture of villains, and sports featuring cruelty to animals.

Violence is pervasive even in a society as advanced as modern-day America. Professor Tricia Rose explains:

> Throughout the twentieth century especially, violence was wedded to mainstream visions of manhood. . . . The pro-violence, celebratory air associated with military action and action heroes and the fascination with mobsters and other American gangsters, hunting, and the regulated violence that fuels boxing, football, and hockey have saturated American culture. In every case, these expressions of American values celebrate the male who is able and willing to challenge others to battle and be entirely prepared to act violently.[3]

Given our history, some argue that violent entertainment is simply the product of a violent world, not the other way around. One notable example is hip-hop music, a genre that has been criticized for encouraging listeners to engage in criminal behavior. Professor Rose, however, points out that during the 1980s inner cities were flooded with cheap and addictive drugs, especially crack cocaine, which coupled with easy access to guns, including semiautomatic weapons, made

FROM THE BENCH

Eclipse Enterprises, Inc. v. Gulotta, 134 F.3d 63 (2d Cir. 1997)

In 1992, Nassau County, New York, passed an ordinance creating the offense of "disseminating indecent crime material to a minor," which applied to items such as trading cards that depict "a heinous crime, an element of a heinous crime, or a heinous criminal" and are "harmful to minors." The definition of "harmful to minors" mirrored the *Miller* obscenity test, except that the first portion of the test applied to "the depraved interest of minors in crime."

Eclipse Enterprises Inc., the publisher of "true crime" trading cards, challenged the ordinance in federal court. At the trial, the county argued that young people who bought trading cards glorifying crime and criminals would be more likely to imitate what was depicted on the cards. The District Court, however, found "no credible or empirical evidence" supporting that argument and concluded that the ordinance violated the First Amendment.

The county appealed to the U.S. Court of Appeals for the Second Circuit, which affirmed the lower court's ruling in *Eclipse Enterprises, Inc. v. Gulotta*. In the court's opinion, Judge Roger Miner observed that only a few categories of speech— defamation, "fighting words," direct incitement of lawless action, and obscenity—were not protected by the First Amendment and expressed his reluctance to add to the list. Even though the county had declared violent trading cards "harmful to minors," he noted that depictions of violence were protected speech, while obscenity was not.

Although Judge Miner agreed that the county had a compelling interest in protecting young people from psychological harm and in combating juvenile

violent outbursts almost inevitable. At the same time, the government launched the "war on drugs," which targeted African-American communities. The result was a huge increase in the number of African Americans in prison or on parole. Rose goes on to explain: "Hip-hop emerged in this context, and thus the tales of drug dealing, pimping, petty crime, dropping out of school, and joining a gang are more aptly seen as reflections of the violence experienced in these areas than as

---

crime, he said that the county had to offer evidence of real, not conjectural, harm. The court declared that the county failed to meet its burden of proof: Its evidence consisted of "contested studies concerning TV violence, the conclusory and contradictory testimony of its own experts, and conclusory testimony of community activists." Miner also found that the county had failed to explain why trading cards should be regulated while media containing similar content was not regulated. He pointed out that books in the county library, and even some textbooks used in schools, contained descriptions of crimes and criminals that were similar to those found on the trading cards. Finally, given the court's ruling in this case, Miner found it unnecessary to answer the question of whether narrowly tailored restrictions on material that was not obscene but otherwise harmful to minors—especially younger minors—could ever be found constitutional.

While Judge Thomas Griesa agreed that the trading-card ordinance was unconstitutional, he maintained that the case was "closer and less one-sided" than the majority opinion indicated and that a case could be made for putting violence in the same legal category as obscenity. Griesa described some of Eclipse's trading cards, one of which described a murderer having sex with the decapitated body of his victim, and another that described cutting a victim into pieces and making a stew out of the body parts. Such content, in his view, might permissibly be kept from minors. Nevertheless, he concluded that the ordinance, as written, was not limited to the most offensive cards. The phrase "appeals to the depraved interest of minors in crime" was not only too broad, but it also failed to meet the Supreme Court's requirement that prohibited content be specifically defined in a manner similar to the sex acts and body parts spelled out in obscenity laws.

origins of the violence."[4] Hip-hop artists insist they are merely "keeping it real"—that is, describing the often violent side of inner-city life.

The entertainment industry has a long and successful history of self-regulation.

The film industry has regulated itself for a century, and its current film ratings, dating back to 1968, have become a model for other industries. "Parental advisory" labels have appeared on recorded music for more than 20 years, and the video game industry has rated its products for 15 years. Today's rating systems are quite sophisticated. Video game ratings include some 30 descriptors that warn parents of everything from coarse language to depictions of gambling. Broadcasters also alert parents to specific content that might concern them. In 2007, Kevin Martin, the chairman of the Federal Communications Commission (FCC), said:

> The television industry has already developed definitions of violence that [are] used in their ratings system. Specifically, the TV Parental Guidelines developed by the television industry include ratings that indicate the presence of "fantasy violence," "no violence," "moderate violence," "intense violence," and "graphic violence." Thus, it appears that the industry agrees with some basic definition of violence in programming, at least for use with blocking technologies.[5]

The entertainment industry has often been unfairly compared to the tobacco industry. To begin with, every state has a law barring the sale of tobacco to minors. By contrast, age limits for entertainment do not have the force of law. Furthermore, the government concluded in the early 1960s that smoking caused cancer and other diseases (although evidence suggesting a link existed before that), but no federal agency has found a conclusive connection between violent entertainment and real-world violence. We also now know that tobacco companies misled the public by downplaying the risks of smoking-related diseases. On the other hand, the entertainment industry clearly labels adult-rated content.

Some reject the argument that entertainment teaches anti-social behavior. Professor Schechter said:

> Contrary to accusations that they "glorify violence," even hyperkinetic action shows and movies reinforce traditional morality, vilifying the bad guys and celebrating the triumph of virtue. Indeed, if the average Hollywood shoot-'em-up can be criticized for anything, it is for portraying a universe devoid of moral ambiguity, where evil is easily identified and invariably defeated, and the all-American heroes are saints armed with semiautomatic weapons.[6]

In Schechter's view, many films and television shows present an oversimplified view of the world that is even worse than the violence itself. In any event, young people are more sophisticated consumers of entertainment than critics think. In our media-saturated society, they learn early on to distinguish entertainment from the real world and see entertainment as an escape from reality.

Critics are politically and culturally biased.

Many critics do not understand the very entertainment they condemn. For example, they are unaware that the *Grand Theft Auto* video games are satirical in nature: Rather than glorifying violence, they actually make fun of it. Critics also fail to distinguish among violent games. For example, in the game *SWAT 4*, players earn points for *not* killing characters—even the "bad guys"—and for getting medical help for injured characters. Nevertheless, *SWAT 4* has the same violence-related content descriptors as games that reward players for killing characters.

Yet, the same people who attack *Grand Theft Auto* rarely criticize military video games, even though these games often contain brutal violence.

FROM THE BENCH

Video Software Dealers Association v. Schwarzenegger, 556 F.3d 950 (9th Circ. 2009)

In 2005, Governor Arnold Schwarzenegger of California signed legislation banning the sale of violent video games to customers younger than 18 and requiring manufacturers of adult-rated games to place an "18" sticker on them. The law's definition of "violent video game" contained two alternate versions. The first version incorporated the *Miller* obscenity test, as applied to minors. The second applied to games that enabled the player to inflict serious injury on images of human beings in a manner that is "especially heinous, cruel, or depraved in that it involves torture or serious physical abuse to the victim." The law also cited two reasons for restricting violent video games: Exposing young players to those games made them behave more aggressively, and young players who did not commit acts of violence still suffered psychological harm from prolonged exposure to violent games.

Trade associations representing manufacturers and retailers of video games sued to block enforcement of the law. After the District Court agreed with the trade associations, the state appealed to the U.S. Court of Appeals for the Ninth Circuit. On appeal, California argued that the "rational-relationship" test, which the Supreme Court had applied in *Ginsberg v. New York*, should apply in this case because violent video games were as "harmful to minors" as pornography.

In *Video Software Dealers Association v. Schwarzenegger*, the appeals court unanimously rejected California's argument and affirmed the lower court's judgment. Judge Consuelo Callahan, in the court's opinion, concluded that the strict-scrutiny test, not the rational-relationship test, applied to violent games. Judge Callahan noted that other appeals court decisions had come to the same conclusion, and, even though the Supreme Court had not specifically ruled on the issue, she found that story-laden video games were similar to movies, which the Court has long considered protected speech. She also concluded that the Supreme Court had never intended to extend the harmful-to-minors doctrine to violence:

Critics of entertainment often apply a double standard. In the 1992 presidential campaign, President George H.W. Bush condemned the producers of a record that glorified the killing of

---

Ginsberg is specifically rooted in the Court's First Amendment obscenity jurisprudence, which relates to non-protected sex-based expression—not violent content, which is presumably protected by the First Amendment.... The *Ginsberg* Court applied a rational basis test to the statute at issue because it placed the magazines at issue within a sub-category of obscenity—obscenity as to minors—that had been determined to be not protected by the First Amendment, and it did not create an entirely new category of expression excepted from First Amendment protection. The State, in essence, asks us to create a new category of non-protected material based on its depiction of violence.

To prove that violent video games were harmful to young players, California relied on several experts who studied the effects of these games on young players. Callahan, however, found that their work did not establish such harm:

Nearly all of the research is based on correlation, not evidence of causation, and most of the studies suffer from significant, admitted flaws in methodology as they relate to the State's claimed interest. None of the research establishes or suggests a causal link between minors playing violent video games and actual psychological or neurological harm, and inferences to that effect would not be reasonable. In fact, some of the studies caution against inferring causation.

Therefore, the state's evidence failed to demonstrate a compelling interest in preventing psychological or neurological harm to young players. Even if California had demonstrated such an interest, Callahan concluded that an age limit was not the least-restrictive means of furthering it. She suggested one possible less restrictive way of keeping violent games away from young players: an enhanced education campaign by the video game industry.

Finally, Callahan found the law's labeling provision unconstitutional. She concluded that the law's "18" label "does not convey factual information" because California's age limit was unconstitutional, and she added that the proposed label "would arguably now convey a false statement that certain conduct is illegal when it is not."

police officers. At the same time, he welcomed the endorsement of actor Arnold Schwarzenegger who, in the 1984 film *Terminator*, played a character who killed dozens of police officers. In fact, public officials, including Schwarzenegger himself, have also been accused of targeting entertainment for political reasons. As governor of California, Schwarzenegger signed a law restricting young people's access to violent video games, even though courts had struck down similar laws in other states. The California law was later found unconstitutional. Schwarzenegger and other political officials know that "demonizing" entertainment has been popular with voters for years. Attacking entertainment companies also gives voters the impression that the government is doing something about violence in society. At the same time, it deflects attention from the other causes of real-world violence, such as poverty, unemployment, and racial discrimination.

Criticism of entertainment is often motivated by racial and cultural bias. Because jazz, blues, and rock and roll all had their roots in African-American culture, these genres of music were condemned when they first entered mainstream culture. Many observers believe that hip-hop is judged more harshly than other genres of music because the performers are largely black and some of them openly express hostility toward the police and other authority figures. The enforcement of laws regulating entertainment has also been uneven, with members of minority groups more likely to be targeted. Professor Rose cites the case of musician Sarah Jones. In 2001, the FCC threatened to fine a radio station in Oregon for playing Jones's song "Your Revolution." That song was filled with sexual references, but the lyrics were intended as a condemnation of anti-woman messages often found in rap and rock music. Rose argues that the FCC selectively enforced the Broadcast Decency Rule in this case: "This wasn't just a matter of free speech; it was, given the incredible range of explicit and sexist sexuality expressed by men and women in American commercial culture, a direct attack on independent, feminist sexual empowerment cloaked under the language of 'decency.'"[7]

The fears of critics have rarely come true.

The arguments raised against hip-hop music and video games are remarkably similar to those raised earlier against other forms of entertainment. Professor Schechter explains:

> What's so interesting about the antipop campaigns that have now been going on for several hundred years is how exactly alike they are. The pattern is always the same. A new medium of mass entertainment comes along that is aimed at—or embraced primarily by— kids and the working class. Very quickly, high-minded reformers begin to denounce it as a sign of social decay, a corrupter of the young, a threat to the very existence of civilization as we know it.[8]

Schechter insists that the entertainment enjoyed by past generations was even worse. For example, publications that were popular before the Civil War described crime in gory detail and expressed viciously racist sentiments. Yet the dire predictions about the harmful effects of such entertainment rarely come true. In nineteenth-century England, so-called penny dread-fuls—stories heavy with crime and violence—became popular. According to Kutner and Olson, critics soon attacked them: "Victorian society blamed juvenile crime on these cheap publi-cations as well as on the penny gaffs [low-class theatrical produc-tions], and paid little attention to the contributions of poverty, urban migration, and prostitution. In fact, crime was decreasing dramatically in England during the peak of these stories' popu-larity."[9] In 1949, social critic Gershon Legman warned:

> With rare exceptions, every child in America who was six years old in 1938 has by now absorbed an absolute minimum of eighteen thousand pictorial beatings, shootings, stranglings, blood-puddles and torturings-to-death from comic books alone. The effect, if not the

(continues on page 82)

FROM THE BENCH

American Amusement Machine Association v. Kendrick, 244 F.3d 572 (7th Cir. 2001)

In 2000, Indianapolis passed an ordinance that barred people younger than 18 from playing violent video games in public arcades. The ordinance applied to games the city defined as "harmful to minors"—that is, they predominantly appealed to minors' morbid interest in violence; were patently offensive to prevailing standards in the adult community as a whole with respect to what was suitable for those younger than 18; lacked serious literary, artistic, political, or scientific value as a whole for those younger than 18; and contained "graphic violence." Arcade operators who violated the ordinance could be fined or even lose their licenses.

The American Amusement Machine Association filed suit to stop the city from enforcing the ordinance. The case went to the U.S. Court of Appeals for the Seventh Circuit, which in *American Amusement Machine Association v. Kendrick* unanimously found the ordinance unconstitutional. *Kendrick* is believed to be the first published appeals court decision dealing with the constitutionality of video game regulation.

Judge Richard Posner wrote the court's opinion. He first took issue with Indianapolis's equating violent video games with pornography, pointing out that society outlaws obscenity because it is offensive, not because it is harmful. He conceded that some depictions of violence—such as photographs of a person being drawn and quartered—might be offensive enough to be considered obscene, but he noted that Indianapolis wanted to regulate video games because the city considered them harmful to young players. The judge found the city's evidence of the games' harmfulness insufficient to justify regulating them: "The studies do not find that video games have ever caused anyone to commit a violent act, as opposed to feeling aggressive, or have caused the average level of violence to increase anywhere."

In Judge Posner's view, laws aimed at protecting young people from violent entertainment might do more harm than good: "People are unlikely to become well-functioning, independent-minded adults and responsible citizens if they are raised in an intellectual bubble." He added that it was impossible to shield young people from depictions of violence—children have grown up with gruesome fairy tales for centuries—and even if it were possible, doing so would leave them "unequipped to cope with the world as we know it." Judge Posner also found it dangerous for the government to control what young people saw and heard:

A very young boy aims a toy gun at a public arcade game screen. In 2000, the city of Indianapolis passed an ordinance that banned anyone younger than 18 from playing violent video games. Although the U.S. Court of Appeals for the Seventh Circuit overturned the law, it left open the possibility that a more narrowly defined law could be considered constitutional.

"The murderous fanaticism displayed by young German soldiers in World War II, alumni of the Hitler Jugend, illustrates the danger of allowing government to control the access of children to information and opinion."

Posner also rejected the city's argument that video games enjoyed less First Amendment protection than other forms of entertainment because they were "interactive." He observed:

> All literature (here broadly defined to include movies, television, and the other photographic media, and popular as well as highbrow literature) is interactive; the better it is, the more interactive. Literature when it is

(continues)

FROM THE BENCH

(continues)

successful draws the reader into the story, makes him identify with the characters, invites him to judge them and quarrel with them, to experience their joys and sufferings as the reader's own. . . . Some games, such as "Dungeons and Dragons," have achieved cult status; although it seems unlikely, some of these games, perhaps including some that are as violent as those in the record, will become cultural icons. We are in the world of kids' popular culture. But it is not lightly to be suppressed.

Posner stopped short of declaring all laws aimed at protecting young players from violent games as unconstitutional. He left open the possibility that the government might someday offer enough evidence to justify regulating the games—he felt that a narrowly drawn law, aimed at realistic-looking depictions of death and mutilation or "animated shooting galleries" with no storyline, might be held constitutional.

(continued from page 79)

intention, has been to raise up an entire generation of adolescents—twenty million of them—who have felt, thousands upon thousands of times, all the sensations and emotions of committing murder, except pulling the trigger.[10]

When Legman made that statement, however, the arrest rate for teenagers in New York City was only one-fifth what it had been 40 years earlier.

Finally, some forms of entertainment are heavily criticized simply because they are new. In *Entertainment Software Association v. Granholm* (2006), which found Michigan's video game law unconstitutional, the judge suggested that the law discriminated against a disfavored "newcomer" in the world of entertainment media. Several other courts have noted that the same violent content found in video games is widely available in other, more established media that lawmakers have chosen not to regulate. Another common argument against new media—and video games in particular—is that they are "more realistic" and therefore more dangerous. This argument fails to put entertainment into perspective: What today's audiences regard as unconvincing had a powerful effect on the public when it first appeared. Professor Schechter cites the famous 1938 radio drama, *The War of the Worlds*, a fictitious account of an invasion by Martians that was presented on air as a series of news bulletins. Millions of listeners thought that an actual invasion was taking place and, according to newspaper accounts, some reacted with panic.

Violent entertainment can be beneficial.

Contrary to critics' claims, playing video games is more a social activity than a refuge for troubled young people. According to a 2005 survey by the Kaiser Family Foundation, only 18 percent of males and 12 percent of females said they always played video games alone. In fact, *not* playing games might be a danger sign. After the Virginia Tech shootings in 2007, acquaintances said that they had not seen the shooter, Seung-Hui Cho, play video games. Lawrence Kutner and Cheryl K. Olson say that it is highly unusual for young men not to play video games, because they use them to build and strengthen social relationships with their peers. They view Cho's lack of involvement with video games as indication of his poor social skills and his status as a social outcast.

Kutner and Olson also suggest that playing video games can help players later in life. They cite studies that indicate playing video games helped children become better decision-makers and enabled women to hone skills that improved their performance as surgeons, scientists, and engineers. Kutner and Olson's own study found that playing video games helped young players manage their emotions: 62 percent of boys said they played video games to help relax, 48 percent said games helped them forget their problems, and 45 percent said they played games to release their anger. Those findings support the argument that, for some people, violent entertainment provides for the release of violent feelings. Professor Schechter adds, "As psychoanalysis teaches, one of the primary functions of horror stories is to help the audience manage its unspoken fears—cope with profoundly disturbing experiences—by giving them a reassuring narrative shape."[11] Many of the creators of violent comic books were Jewish and had watched films taken at the Nazi death camps. Schechter suggests that drawing gory scenes helped these artists cope with the real-world horror they had seen.

Gerard Jones, an author who overcame his shyness by reading comic books, contends that violent entertainment can help young people adjust to the world:

> At its most fundamental level, what we call "creative violence"—head-bonking cartoons, bloody video games, playground karate, toy guns—gives children a tool to master their rage. . . . Through immersion in imaginary combat and identification with a violent protagonist, children engage the rage they've stifled, come to fear it less, and become more capable of utilizing it against life's challenges.[12]

Jones adds that, if we suppress violent entertainment, we risk confusing children about their natural aggression in the same way that parents of the Victorian era suppressed their children's natural sexuality.

Summary
Critics unjustly blame the entertainment industry for crime and other social problems. The entertainment industry has a long and successful history of self-regulation. Criticisms of modern forms of entertainment are almost identical to those raised in the past against now-mainstream entertainment. Accusations that violent

entertainment causes real-world crime and violence have repeatedly been proven wrong; in fact, violent entertainment reflects our violent culture, not the other way around. Critics of popular culture are often motivated by political opportunism and cultural bias, and tend to be overly suspicious of unfamiliar forms of entertainment such as video games. Some experts maintain that entertainment can help people form friendships, develop skills, and come to terms with their own violent nature.

Regulating Entertainment Is Necessary

In the 2006 film *Hostel*, travelers are lured by the promise of sex and drugs to a European youth hostel and turned over to wealthy sadists who have paid tens of thousands of dollars for the privilege of torturing them to death. Despite its extremely graphic content—one critic called the film "torture porn"—the Motion Picture Association of America (MPAA) gave the film an R rating, meaning that people younger than 17 could see it with a parent. Robert Peters, the president of Morality in Media Inc., reacted to the rating decision:

> [D]oes the MPAA really think *Hostel* is suitable entertainment for even young children, as long as a parent accompanies them? Does the MPAA also think *Hostel* is suitable entertainment for impressionable and often vulnerable 17-year-old high school juniors, even when

unaccompanied by a parent? Is it possible that the MPAA is also unaware that many theaters are lax in their enforcement of the R-rating? Does it give a darn?[1]

Some entertainment is harmful.

American media have been called the world's most violent. In fact, some of the graphic violent entertainment our young people are exposed to would not be acceptable in other Western countries. Lawrence Kutner and Cheryl K. Olson note that, under the European-wide rating system, video games that frighten players or encourage discrimination earn more restrictive ratings. They also quote a German regulator who told them, "In America, sex and bad language seems to be the focus of discussion. . . . Here in Germany, violence dominates our concerns, and too much violence can get a game banned."[2] In *Miramax Films Corporation v. Motion Picture Association of America* (1990), a rare legal challenge to the MPAA's film ratings, the judge criticized the ratings for being too tolerant of "hard violence," and suggested that the industry had put profits ahead of the welfare of young filmgoers.

Some critics, including the Federal Communications Commission (FCC), compare violent entertainment to "fighting words," which, as the Supreme Court said in the 1942 case of *Chaplinsky v. New Hampshire*, had such slight social value that the government could regulate them without violating the First Amendment. These same critics also contend that judges should have paid more attention to Justice Felix Frankfurter's dissenting opinion in *Winters v. New York* (1948), in which he argued that the "true crime" publications in that case not only lacked social value, but were actually harmful to society. Such critics believe that the *Winters* decision and Supreme Court decisions that followed it have led to a result the framers of the Constitution never intended. Columnist Gregg Easterbrook explains:

(continues on page 90)

THE LETTER OF THE LAW

The Broadcast Decency Rule

Some proposals to regulate violent entertainment are modeled after the Broadcast Decency Rule, which governs radio and broadcast television. The rule is an outgrowth of a law, on the books since 1927, that makes it illegal to broadcast "obscene, indecent, or profane" language. The Federal Communications Commission (FCC), which regulates broadcasting, has strictly enforced that rule.

In 1973, a citizen complained to the FCC that WBAI-FM, a New York radio station, had broadcast "Seven Words You Can Never Say on Television," a satirical monologue by comedian George Carlin. The FCC found Carlin's monologue "indecent"—it contained "language or material that, in context, depicts or describes, in terms patently offensive as measured by contemporary community standards for the broadcast medium, sexual or excretory activities or organs." Because WBAI broadcast the monologue in the afternoon, when young people were likely to be in the audience, the FCC ruled that it had broken the law. The Pacifica Foundation, WBAI's owner, appealed the FCC's ruling. That appeal reached the Supreme Court, which, in *Federal Communications Commission v. Pacifica Foundation*, 438 U.S. 726 (1978), ruled five to four in favor of the FCC.

Justice John Paul Stevens wrote the Court's opinion. He first concluded that the FCC had the authority to regulate material that was not legally obscene. He cited two reasons why broadcast media had a lower level of First Amendment protection than other media. First, "the broadcast media have established a uniquely pervasive presence in the lives of all Americans." Thus, indecent material had the ability to invade the privacy of the home; and, since the audience was constantly tuning in and out, prior warnings were not sufficient to protect listeners from unexpected content. Second, broadcasts were "uniquely accessible to children," even those too young to read. Justice Stevens also pointed out that the Broadcast Decency Rule did not ban indecent material from the airwaves altogether but instead "channeled" it into hours when young people were unlikely to be listening.

Justice William Brennan wrote a dissenting opinion. He argued that Carlin's monologue did not violate listeners' privacy because those who found it offensive could turn it off. He also contended that the Broadcast Decency Rule ignored the constitutional rights of adult listeners and was so broad that it "could justify the banning from radio of a myriad of literary works, novels, poems, and plays by the likes of Shakespeare, Joyce, Hemingway, Ben Johnson, Henry Fielding, Robert Burns, and Chaucer; they could support the suppression of a good deal of political speech, such as the Nixon tapes; and they could even provide the basis for imposing sanctions for the broadcast of certain portions of the Bible."

Pacifica resolved one legal controversy but triggered another one, which lasted for years. Finally, in *Action for Children's Television v. Federal Communications Commission*, 58 F.3d 654 (D.C. Cir. 1995), the U.S. Court of Appeals for the District of Columbia ruled that it was constitutional for the FCC to limit indecent content to the hours between 10 P.M. and 6 A.M. Judge James Buckley, who wrote the majority opinion, stated that the government had a compelling interest in protecting young audiences from indecent broadcasts:

> It is evident beyond the need for elaboration that a State's interest in safeguarding the physical and psychological well-being of a minor is compelling. A democratic society rests, for its continuance, upon the healthy, well-rounded growth of young people into full maturity as citizens. Accordingly, we have sustained legislation aimed at protecting the physical and emotional well-being of youth even when the laws have operated in the sensitive area of constitutionally protected rights.

He also noted that changing public attitudes had narrowed the class of what is obscene but, at the same time, had expanded the category of "indecent" content. Judge Buckley found that the rule helped parents control what their children were exposed to: "It is fanciful to believe that the vast majority of parents who wish to shield their children from indecent material can effectively do so without meaningful restrictions on the airing of broadcast indecency." Finally, Judge Buckley concluded that the Broadcast Decency Rule was the "least restrictive means" of protecting young people from exposure to indecent content, and he said that any inconvenience the rule caused adults was necessary to protect young audiences.

The Broadcast Decency Rule remains on the books. In fact, after Janet Jackson's infamous "wardrobe malfunction" at the 2004 Super Bowl and a number of incidents involving offensive broadcasts by radio "shock jocks," Congress increased the maximum fines that the FCC may impose on violators.

(continued from page 87)

Today, Hollywood and television have twisted the First Amendment concept that occasional repulsive or worthless expression must be protected, so as to guarantee freedom for works of genuine political content or artistic merit, into a new standard in which constitutional freedoms are employed mainly to safeguard works that make no pretense of merit. In the new standard, the bulk of what's being protected is repulsive or worthless, with the meritorious work the rare exception.[3]

In fact, some free-speech experts warn that, if the entertainment industry keeps pushing the boundaries of free expression, that behavior could undermine public support for the First Amendment, including its protection of political speech.

Finally, advocates accuse lawmakers of being too reluctant to regulate violent entertainment and defend those regulations in court, noting that the Supreme Court has never definitively ruled that laws treating violent entertainment as "harmful to minors" are unconstitutional. In *Eclipse Enterprises, Inc. v. Gulotta* (1997), a case involving "true crime" trading cards, a federal appeals court noted that the government had the power to combat juvenile crime and to protect young people from psychological harm. Thomas Griesa, a judge on that court, argued that a properly written law could define some violent entertainment as harmful to minors. In *American Amusement Machine Association v. Kendrick* (2001), an early case involving video game regulation, Judge Richard Posner suggested that some depictions of violence were so offensive that they could be found obscene. Posner, like Griesa, said that a carefully written law, regulating the most extreme violence, might be constitutional. Other regulation advocates believe it is only a matter of time before the scientific evidence becomes overwhelming enough to convince judges that regulation is appropriate and necessary. They point out, for example, that it took scientists many years to convince the courts that smoking was harmful.

Society must protect young people from harm.
Numerous laws, ranging from limits on child labor to safety standards for toys, have been passed to protect children from physical and emotional harm. The courts have long recognized that some entertainment is more harmful to children and teenagers than to adults. In *Ginsberg v. New York* (1968), the Supreme Court upheld state laws setting an age limit for material considered harmful to minors. The Court's opinion quoted from a law review article explaining that material was harmful:

> It is in the period of growth [of youth] when these patterns of behavior are laid down, when environmental stimuli of all sorts must be integrated into a workable sense of self, when sensuality is being defined and fears elaborated, when pleasure confronts security and impulse encounters control—it is in this period, undramatically and with time, that legalized pornography may conceivably be damaging.[4]

The well-being of young people was also one of the reasons why the courts upheld the Broadcast Decency Rule, which "channels" indecent broadcasts into the nighttime hours when the audience consists primarily of adults. In 2007, the FCC gave unanimous support to extending the rule to "excessively violent" programming. In doing so, it explained: "Just as the government has a compelling interest in protecting children from sexually explicit programming, a strong argument can be made ... that the government also has a compelling interest in protecting children from violent programming and supporting parental supervision of minors' viewing of violent programming."[5]

Why is it so important to protect minors from violent entertainment? Scientists have discovered that a person's brain is not fully "wired" until he or she reaches adulthood. During the teenage years, the brain's "executive function" is still undeveloped: A person exhibits less self-control; is not as capable of controlling impulses and emotions; and is still learning to organize, plan, and set goals. Professor Kevin W. Saunders comments:

> It is becoming clear that the environment in which the teenager lives has physical effects on that teenager's

Should Violent Television Content Be "Channeled?"

In March 2005, 39 members of Congress asked the Federal Communications Commission (FCC) to determine whether it would be appropriate to "channel" violent programming into hours when young viewers were unlikely to be in the audience and whether doing so would be constitutional. Two years later, the FCC issued a report, which all five commissioners voted to approve.

Part II of the report, which dealt with the effects of violent programs on young viewers, concluded: "Given the totality of the record before us, we agree with the view of the Surgeon General that: 'a diverse body of research provides strong evidence that exposure to violence in the media can increase children's aggressive behavior in the short term.' At the same time, we do recognize that 'many questions remain regarding the short- and long-term effects of media violence, especially on violent behavior.'"

In Part III, the FCC found that it would be constitutional to channel violent programming into the nighttime hours, as it did with indecent programming:

> Just as the government has a compelling interest in protecting children from sexually explicit programming, a strong argument can be made ... that the government also has a compelling interest in protecting children from violent programming and supporting parental supervision of minors' viewing of violent programming. We also believe that, if properly defined, excessively violent programming, like indecent programming, occupies a relatively low position in the hierarchy of First Amendment values because it is of "slight social value as a step to truth."

The FCC also concluded that the broadcasting industry's voluntary rating system should be replaced with a mandatory system. A mandatory rating system

brain development. This demonstrates a route through which environmental factors cause later behavior and that the environmental causes occur throughout the teenage years. The influences to which a child is exposed do matter. The remaining issue is that of who should be allowed to provide that input.[6]

"could be defended on the grounds that it merely requires the disclosure of truthful information about a potentially harmful product (violent television programming), thereby advancing the compelling government interests without significantly burdening First Amendment rights. It could also be defended as a necessary predicate for the operation of a successful system of viewer-initiated blocking." However, the commissioners cautioned that mandatory ratings "would not fully serve the government's interest in the well-being of minors," given the limits of parental supervision recognized by the federal courts.

In Part IV, the FCC acknowledged the broadcasting industry's concerns about an overly broad definition of "violence" but concluded that it was possible to define violence in a way that gave the industry fair warning. Such a definition "might cover depictions of physical force against an animate being that, in context, are patently offensive. In determining whether such depictions are patently offensive, the Government could consider among other factors the presence of weapons, whether the violence is extensive or graphic, and whether the violence is realistic."

Even though he voted to approve the report, Commissioner Jonathan Adelstein expressed unease with the channeling proposal. He said that channeling would raise constitutional questions and that any regulation capable of standing up in court would likely apply to only a small amount of the violence shown on television. He contended that parents already had a variety of technological tools for controlling what their children watched and called on the government and broadcasters to do more to educate parents about them. Adelstein also said that the amount of violence had dramatically increased during the same time the industry consolidated and blamed his fellow commissioners for allowing the broadcasting industry to end up in so few hands.

Source: *In the Matter of Violent Television Programming and its Impact On Children*, No. FCC 07-50 (Federal Communications Commission, April 25, 2007).

It follows that exposure to violent entertainment—especially interactive media such as video games—has a more profound effect on young people than on adults.

Some argue that the consequences of mistakenly regulating violent entertainment are slight since young people will be denied access to only materials that have minimal social value. By contrast, the consequences of *not* regulating that entertainment are great: Juvenile crime rates increase, and young people develop psychological problems resulting from exposure to graphic violence. So far, the courts have been too timid about regulation. They insist that scientists not only show that entertainment is harmful but also rule out other possible causes of real-world violence. Some fear that the courts' approach will be costly. If violent entertainment is as harmful as the public health community believes, society could pay a high price for years to come.

Minors have fewer constitutional rights than adults.

The law classifies those younger than a given age—in most states, age 18—as minors. Minors cannot make certain decisions for themselves, such as signing a contract or enlisting in the military. In addition, the law imposes an age limit for a variety of activities, such as drinking and gambling. The purpose of age limits is to discourage young people from making harmful decisions, such as taking up smoking, and to minimize the risk of their harming others, for example, by driving drunk and causing a traffic crash. Many regulation advocates, including Professor Saunders, support age limits for violent entertainment as well as other material that might be harmful. Saunders argues that society should protect young people from such material for the same reason it sends young offenders to juvenile court rather than adult court. In both cases, different legal treatment is justified because young people are not "fully formed."

The courts have long recognized that young people have fewer constitutional rights than adults. For example, school

administrators can require student-athletes to take drug tests
in order to stay eligible for competition and search students on
a lesser degree of probable cause that the police need to search
an adult, and communities can pass youth curfews and set age
limits for entering certain places of entertainment. Young people
have limited First Amendment rights as well. In *Ginsberg*, the
Supreme Court said:

> The world of children is not strictly part of the adult
> realm of free expression. . . . Without attempting here to
> formulate the principles relevant to freedom of expres-
> sion for children, it suffices to say that regulations of
> communication addressed to them need not conform
> to the requirements of the First Amendment in the
> same way as those applicable to adults.[7]

One reason for limiting young peoples' First Amendment
rights is that they are not yet able to choose wisely in the
so-called marketplace of ideas. In any event, entertainment
does less to help young people become informed citizens than
political speech.

Age limits also reinforce parents' authority to raise their
children as they see fit. As the Court noted in *Ginsberg*: "The
legislature could properly conclude that parents and others,
teachers for example, who have this primary responsibility for
children's well-being are entitled to the support of laws designed
to aid discharge of that responsibility."[8] Since then, the parents'
gatekeeper role has been undermined by entertainment companies marketing their products directly to young audiences.
Saunders argues:

> A musical group or a motion picture production com-
> pany should have no right to insist that its offerings
> be directly available to children to help those children
> eventually see the truth. That argument may hold for

adults, but parents should have the right to determine the factors that contribute to the psychological development of their children. They may choose to allow their

---

FROM THE BENCH

Miramax Films Corporation v. Motion Picture Association of America, Inc., 148 Misc. 2d 1, 560 N.Y.S.2d 730 (Sup. Ct., New York County 1990)

In 1968, the Motion Picture Association of America (MPAA) instituted an age-based system for rating films. The most restrictive rating was X, meaning that no one younger than 17 could be admitted. Only a few mainstream films received an X rating. One of them was *Tie Me Up! Tie Me Down!*, a 1990 film directed by Spain's Pedro Almodovar that earned the rating on account of several sexually explicit scenes.

An X rating was economically damaging to a mainstream film because many theaters and video stores refused to handle it. The rating was also associated with pornographic films, which were often advertised as XXX,—an unintended result of the MPAA's failure to copyright the X rating. Rather than make changes to *Tie Me Up!* that would earn it a less-restrictive R rating, Miramax Films Corporation released the film without a rating, and challenged the MPAA's decision in court. In *Miramax Films Corporation v. Motion Picture Association of America, Inc.*, Justice Charles Ramos ruled in favor of the MPAA.

Because the MPAA was a private organization, not a government agency, Judge Ramos applied a very low level of scrutiny—namely, whether the association had acted "arbitrarily and capriciously." He found that Miramax had failed to prove clear and intentional discrimination or bad faith on the MPAA's part and found no support for Miramax's allegations that the MPAA was biased against foreign films and independent distributors.

Even though he ruled in the MPAA's favor, Ramos called the association's rating system "an effective form of censorship" because it governed content that was not legally obscene. He also said that the rating system was seriously flawed, not just with respect to *Tie Me Up!* but to films in general, and found that those who rated films lacked expertise. The MPAA instructed members of ratings boards to judge a film based on the tastes of the "average American parent," but required no special qualifications. The "average American parent" standard, in Ramos's

children to hear the music or see the film at issue, but restrictions on sales or rentals to children should be upheld in support of the parents' rights.[9]

view, was unscientific: "There are no physicians, child psychiatrists, or child-care professionals on the board, nor is any professional guidance sought to advise the board members regarding any relative harm to minor children. No effort is made to professionally advise the board members on the impact of a depiction of violent rape on the one hand and an act of love on the other, nor is any distinction made between levels of violence."

Ramos also criticized as "indefensible" the MPAA's tolerance of film violence. He quoted an MPAA memo that reminded board members to "remember always how much violence seems to be accepted, perhaps even expected, in television and films." He went on to observe that "the MPAA ratings are skewed towards permitting filmmakers huge profits pandering to the appetite for films containing 'hard violence' and 'drug use' while neglecting the welfare of children intended to be protected by the rating system."

In addition, Ramos rejected the MPAA's argument that sole purpose of an X rating was to "avoid psychological abuse of children." He responded: "The industry that profits from scenes of mass murder, dismemberment, and the portrayal of war as noble and glamorous apparently has no interest in the opinions of professionals, only the opinions of its consumers."

Finally, Ramos called on the MPAA to "strongly consider some changes in its methods of operations," warning that if the association failed to do so, it could face a "viable legal challenge" from those adversely affected by rating decisions, "including organizations charged with the responsibility of protecting children." He also "strongly advised" the MPAA to either establish "a professional basis" for rating films or get out of the film-rating business altogether.

A postscript. The same year Judge Ramos handed down the *Miramax* opinion, the MPAA replaced the X rating with NC-17, which also imposed an adults-only age restriction but was not associated with pornography.

Source: *Miramax Films Corporation v. Motion Picture Association of America, Inc.*, 148 Misc. 2d 1, 560 N.Y.S.2d 730 (N.Y. Sup. Ct., New York County 1990).

Courts are thwarting society's efforts to protect young people.

The "strict-scrutiny" standard, under which laws regulating speech are often found unconstitutional, is a relatively recent legal development. Until the Supreme Court began to apply that standard, courts typically deferred to lawmakers' determination that certain entertainment was harmful, especially to young people. One notable example was the *Ginsberg* decision, which upheld New York's harmful-to-minors law. The majority opinion in that case quoted New York's highest court, which had observed:

> To be sure, there is no lack of "studies" which purport to demonstrate that obscenity is or is not "a basic factor in impairing the ethical and moral development of . . . youth and a clear and present danger to the people of the state." But the growing consensus of commentators is that "while these studies all agree that a causal link has not been demonstrated, they are equally agreed that a causal link has not been disproved either."[10]

Supporters of regulation believe that the "rational-basis" standard is the correct one to use when reviewing laws restricting violent entertainment. They believe courts should not second-guess lawmakers' reasons for regulating entertainment or their choice of regulatory tools.

Advocates believe that the Supreme Court's application of the strict-scrutiny standard focuses too much on the rights of speakers, many of which are large corporations that sell entertainment for profit, and downplays society's interest in the welfare of its citizens. They contend that strict scrutiny makes it almost impossible for lawmakers to write laws that are specific enough to satisfy the courts. Others argue that it requires the government to come forward with scientific evidence that may never be found. Saunders explains:

Studies involving exposure to violence necessarily involve a variety of depictions. A laboratory study of short-term effects may focus on a particular type of depiction, but real-world studies of general exposure to violence and long-term effect are just that: general. Children cannot be placed in different groups and exposed only to particular types of violence over an extended period to determine the effects of each variety. Only general conclusions can be reached regarding the overall effects of violence. Yet, without this unacceptable variety of experiment, the "narrow tailoring" requirement will be unmet.[11]

Advocates of regulation also insist that the available scientific evidence, combined with common sense and everyday experience, already make a powerful case in favor of regulation. Some even argue that the entertainment industry should be required to prove that violent entertainment is *not* harmful.

Finally, advocates accuse courts of demanding an unreasonable level of specificity. For example, Michigan's law regulating violent video games had detailed definitions of both "extreme and loathsome violence" and "harmful to minors," yet a federal court still found it unconstitutional. The frustration felt by the drafters of such laws echoes Justice Frankfurter's dissenting opinion in *Winters*:

> What standard of definiteness does the Court furnish the New York legislature in finding indefiniteness in the present law? . . . Should the New York legislature spell out in detail the ingredients of stories or pictures which accomplish such "inciting"? What is there in the condemned law that leaves men in the dark as to what is meant by publications that exploit "criminal deeds of bloodshed or lust" thereby "inciting violent and depraved crimes"?[12]

Summary

Some of today's entertainment has minimal social value and might even do more harm than good. Nevertheless, there are few legal restrictions on its distribution and marketing. Recent court rulings have overturned laws regulating violent entertainment because courts use a demanding standard, called strict scrutiny, when reviewing laws that affect speech. Under strict scrutiny, judges have rejected scientific evidence linking violent entertainment to real-world crime and insisted on an unreasonable amount of specificity from lawmakers. Strict scrutiny ignores society's interests in protecting young people and reducing violent crime. A lower standard of review, like that originally used to uphold harmful-to-minors laws, is more appropriate to use when reviewing laws aimed at protecting young people from violent entertainment and other harmful content.

Regulating Entertainment Is Bad Policy

The 2001 case of *American Amusement Machine Association v. Kendrick* is believed to be the first appeals court decision that dealt specifically with the constitutionality of video game regulation. Judge Richard Posner, who wrote that opinion, observed that violence and art have been inseparable: "Violence has always been and remains a central interest of humankind and a recurrent, even obsessive theme of culture both high and low. It engages the interest of children from an early age, as anyone familiar with the classic fairy tales collected by Grimm, Andersen, and Perrault are aware."[1] Regulation of violent entertainment not only raises constitutional questions but could also do more harm than good, even to the young people the regulations are intended to protect.

Entertainment is constitutionally protected speech.

In the previously mentioned cases of *Winters v. New York* and *Joseph Burstyn, Inc. v. Wilson*, the Supreme Court ruled that entertainment was a form of expression protected by the First Amendment. The reasoning of those cases has since been extended to newer media, such as video games. In *Kendrick*, Judge Posner noted that even though video games were "interactive" and could lead to a variety of outcomes, they had one similarity to older media: They told a story. Because video games, along with recorded music and images on the Internet, are protected speech, the government must meet a demanding standard to justify regulation. Applying a lower standard of review to laws regulating violent entertainment could result in the creation of a new category of speech that is not protected by the First Amendment. The Supreme Court has recognized only a few such categories and has expressed its reluctance to add to that list. For example, in 2008, a federal appeals court overturned a law that banned the distribution of videos depicting cruelty to animals. In doing so, the court said: "[O]utside of patently offensive speech that appeals to the prurient interest, the First Amendment does not require speech to have serious value in order for it to fall under the First Amendment umbrella. What this view overlooks is the great spectrum between speech utterly without social value and high value speech."[2] It is worth noting that "prurient interest" has a specific legal meaning—an abnormal and degrading interest in sex—and is not associated with violence.

Some supporters of regulation argue that violent entertainment is comparable to obscenity, yet most courts have rejected that analogy. In *Kendrick*, Posner explained:

> The main worry about obscenity, the main reason for its proscription, is not that it is harmful . . . but that it is offensive. A work is classified as obscene not upon proof

that it is likely to affect anyone's conduct, but upon proof that it violates community norms regarding the permissible scope of depictions of sexual or sex-related activity.[3]

In *Video Software Dealers Association v. Schwarzenegger,* another federal appeals court stated that the Supreme Court limited obscenity law to sexual content only and noted that several other appeals courts had come to a similar conclusion, finding that the harmful-to-minors doctrine could not be extended to violence.

The mere fact that some people find violent entertainment offensive is no reason to strip it of First Amendment protection. In fact, some argue that unpopular speech is more deserving of protection than popular speech. Hilary Rosen, the president of the Recording Industry Association of America, told a Senate committee investigating the entertainment industry: "After all, the test of whether America allows free speech is not whether it grants freedom to those with whom we mildly disagree. It is whether we protect the freedom of those whose views—and language—make us apoplectic."[4] Vigorous enforcement of the First Amendment protects non-mainstream entertainment from being suppressed by those who find it offensive. In some cases, those who want to suppress entertainment are small in number but well organized. For example, conservative advocacy groups have, on a number of occasions, flooded the Federal Communications Commission (FCC) with complaints about television shows. Those complaints forced the FCC to investigate the shows for possible indecency violations.

Regulation infringes on individual rights.
Those who favor regulation often base their proposals on two restrictions of speech that the Supreme Court has found constitutional. The first restriction is the Broadcast Decency Rule, which limits indecent programming to nighttime hours. Some,

however, insist that this rule intrudes on parents' traditional role as the primary censors of their children's entertainment. In the 1995 case of *Action for Children's Television v. Federal Communications Commission,* Chief Judge Harry Edwards of the U.S. Court of Appeals for the District of Columbia argued in his dissenting opinion:

FROM THE BENCH

James v. Meow Media, Inc., 300 F.3d 683 (6th Cir. 2002)

One legal tool for ridding the marketplace of dangerous products is the product liability lawsuit, in which the victim asks a court to order the manufacturer of a product to compensate him or her for damages the product caused. Some members of the legal community have gone to court on behalf of victims of crimes allegedly caused by exposure to violent entertainment. One such case was *James v. Meow Media, Inc.,* which arose out of a school shooting in West Paducah, Kentucky, in 1997. Michael Carneal, a freshman at the school, walked into the lobby and shot several of his fellow students, killing three and wounding many others. After the shootings, investigators discovered that Carneal had regularly played first-person video games (in which the player shoots at virtual opponents); had a videotape of the movie *The Basketball Diaries,* which contains a dream scene in which a student kills his teacher and several of his classmates; and visited pornography Web sites.

The families of the three slain students sued the manufacturers of the video games and producers of other entertainment that allegedly influenced Carneal to carry out the shootings. They argued that the entertainment companies were negligent because they distributed material they should have known would cause people like Carneal to react violently. The District Court dismissed the families' lawsuit, and the U.S. Court of Appeals for the Sixth Circuit affirmed that decision.

In the appeals court's opinion, Judge Danny Boggs concluded that the entertainment companies could not be held liable for distributing a defective product. Even though the courts had allowed bystanders to sue if they were injured as a direct result of a defective product, such as an exploding bottle, this case involved Carneal's *reaction* to the products. Furthermore, the real targets of this lawsuit

Simply put, among the myriad of American parents, not every parent will decide, as the Commission has, that the best way to raise its child is to have the Government shield children under 18 from indecent broadcasts. Furthermore, not every parent will agree with the Commission's definition of indecency, nor whether it is

were the ideas and images that had influenced Carneal, and product-liability law applied only to tangible objects.

Boggs also concluded that the entertainment companies were not negligent. Negligence law requires a party to use ordinary care to prevent *foreseeable* harm. The shootings in this case, however, were not foreseeable. He explained:

> It appears simply impossible to predict that these games, movies, and Internet sites (alone, or in what combinations) would incite a young person to violence. Carneal's reaction to the games and movies at issue here, assuming that his violent actions were such a reaction, was simply too idiosyncratic to expect the defendants to have anticipated it. We find that it is simply too far a leap from shooting characters on a video screen (an activity undertaken by millions) to shooting people in a classroom (an activity undertaken by a handful, at most) for Carneal's actions to have been reasonably foreseeable to the manufacturers of the media that Carneal played and viewed.

Boggs added that the victims' deaths resulted from an intentional criminal act, which the law considers a "superseding" cause that shifts liability to the criminal actor. In addition, he warned that holding the entertainment companies liable would raise First Amendment concerns. If entertainment companies had to defend their products in a civil case, the social value of those products—an important argument in free-speech cases—would not be a valid defense. In addition, a jury verdict against an entertainment company would force the rest of the industry to guess what it needed to do to avoid being sued. Boggs added that restricting violent video games was better left to state legislatures: Lawmakers were democratically elected, and any restrictions would be spelled out in advance rather than after the fact.

appropriate in some contexts, nor at what age their own children may be exposed to such programming.[5]

Some critics also contend that the Broadcast Decency Rule is a step toward re-establishing the discredited *Hicklin* rule, under which the government could limit adults' access to entertainment in the name of protecting young people from harm.

The second restriction is harmful-to-minors laws. Supporters argue that these laws reinforce parents' efforts to control their children's entertainment choices, especially today, when so many inappropriate choices are widely available. This argument, however, has troubled some judges. In *Interactive Digital Software Association v. St. Louis County* (2002), which struck down a county ordinance regulating violent video games, a federal appeals court observed:

> We do not mean to denigrate the government's role in supporting parents, or the right of parents to control their children's exposure to graphically violent materials. We merely hold that the government cannot silence protected speech by wrapping itself in the cloak of parental authority.... To accept the County's broadly-drawn interest as a compelling one would be to invite legislatures to undermine the First Amendment rights of minors willy-nilly under the guise of promoting parental authority.[6]

Harmful-to-minors laws raise other concerns because some are so broadly written that they could deny young people access to material with social value, such as depictions of war crimes or information about sexual health. Furthermore, they often create a single broad category of "minors" and fail to distinguish those close to the age of majority from those in much earlier stages of development. Critics also insist that there is no logical limit to what is "harmful to minors." They warn that discussions of suicide, advertisements for beer, and even coverage of dangerous sports could fit into this category.

Regulations will not be enforced fairly or sensibly.

It is difficult to write a regulation that provides fair warning of what violence is acceptable because there is no single definition of "violence." The Media Institute recently observed that a Road Runner cartoon, the film *Schindler's List*, an episode of *The Three Stooges*, and a crime story on the evening news all contain violence—yet the violence in each serves a completely different function because of the context in which it is presented. The National Association of Broadcasters told the Federal Communications Commission: "[I]f the definition of violence from the National Television Violence Study were used to regulate television programming, many of the most popular shows in television history, such as *Hill Street Blues*, *Gunsmoke*, and *The Untouchables*, would have been subject to some type of government restriction."[7] Even if it were possible to separate "good" violence from "bad," opponents of regulation contend that it makes more sense to speak out forcefully against bad violence than try to suppress it.

Regulation of speech has unintended consequences. The American Civil Liberties Union (ACLU) has compared censorship to poison gas—a weapon that can blow back and harm you if the wind shifts. The ACLU warns that, once the government starts regulating speech, there is no telling where that regulation might end. During the nineteenth century, supporters of obscenity laws insisted that they would be used only against the most offensive material, yet that is not what happened. The government put antiobscenity advocate Anthony Comstock in charge of enforcing the law. Comstock ordered vast amounts of publications seized and had thousands of people arrested. In his home state of New York, Comstock was also the force behind a law banning depictions of crime—the same law that was over-

(continues on page 110)

Michigan's Law Regulating Video Games

Michigan was one of a number of states that passed laws aimed at keeping violent video games away from young players. Part II of that law was aimed at "ultraviolent explicit video games." With respect to those games, the legislature found:

(a) Published research overwhelmingly finds that ultraviolent explicit video games are harmful to minors because minors who play ultraviolent explicit video games are consistently more likely to exhibit violent, asocial, or aggressive behavior and have feelings of aggression.

(b) Spokespersons for not less than 6 major national health associations have concluded and testified that after reviewing more than 1,000 studies, the studies "point overwhelmingly to a causal connection between media violence and aggressive behavior in some children," concluding that the effects of media violence on minors "are measurable and long-lasting."

(c) Law enforcement officers testified that recent statewide targeted enforcement efforts reveal that minors are capable of purchasing, and do purchase, ultraviolent explicit video games.

(d) Law enforcement officers testified about cases of minors acting out ultraviolent explicit video game behaviors by victimizing other citizens.

(e) The state has a legitimate and compelling interest in safeguarding both the physical and psychological well-being of minors.

(f) The state has a legitimate and compelling interest in preventing violent, aggressive, and asocial behavior from manifesting itself in minors.

(g) The state has a legitimate and compelling interest in directly and substantially alleviating the real-life harms perpetrated by minors who play ultraviolent explicit video games.

For a game to fall within the law's coverage, it had to meet two criteria. The first was that it was an "ultraviolent explicit video game," defined as a video game that continually and repetitively depicts "extreme and loathsome violence." A section of the law, in turn, defined "extreme and loathsome violence" as graphic depictions of physical injuries or violence against parties who realistically appear to be human beings, including actions causing death, inflicting cruelty, dismemberment, decapitation, maiming, disfigurement, or other mutilation of body parts, murder, criminal sexual conduct, or torture.

The second criterion was that the game be "harmful to minors," which the law defined as having all of the following characteristics:

(i) Considered as a whole, the game appeals to the morbid interest in asocial, aggressive behavior of minors as determined by "contemporary local community standards."—that is, a morbid interest in committing uncontrolled aggression against an individual. In determining whether an ultraviolent explicit video game appeals to this interest, the game must be judged with reference to average 16-year-olds.

(ii) The game is patently offensive to contemporary local community standards of adults as to what is suitable for minors.

(iii) Considered as a whole, the game lacks serious literary, artistic, political, educational, or scientific value for minors.

The law provided that disseminating an ultra-violent explicit game to a minor was a civil infraction, punishable by a fine of up to $5,000 for a first offense, up to $15,000 for a second offense, and up to $40,000 for a third or subsequent offense. However, it was a misdemeanor to falsely represent oneself as a minor's parent or guardian or that a minor was at least 17 years old; and it was also a misdemeanor for the manager of game store to knowingly allow a minor to play an ultra-violent explicit game.

One section of the law provided that a parent, a guardian, an immediate family member, or an adult in whose residence the minor is a guest, could allow a minor to play an ultra-violent explicit game. It also allowed an adult to provide an ultra-violent explicit game to a minor for a legitimate medical, scientific, governmental, or judicial purpose.

Another section of the law established the defense of good faith, which a person had to in court if charged with a violation. Good faith existed if the minor showed valid-looking identification that showed him or to her to be at least 17 years old, or the provider of the game had an age-verification requirement; the provider had no independent knowledge that the customer was underage; and the provider complied with the video game industry's rating system.

Despite the lawmakers' reasons for passing it, and its detailed definitions of "harmful to minors," the law was found unconstitutional by a federal judge in *Entertainment Software Association v. Granholm*, 426 F. Supp. 2d 646 (E.D. Mich. 2006).

Source: Act No. 108, Michigan Public Acts of 2005.

(continued from page 107)
turned in *Winters*. At first, the law applied only to distributing crime-oriented material to minors. At Comstock's insistence, the legislature extended the law to adults.

Some view regulation as a form of prohibition, which tends to breed disrespect for the law. When the United States prohibited alcohol from 1920 to 1933, many Americans found alcohol *more* attractive because of its "forbidden fruit" status. It is also questionable whether, given today's technology, regulations are even enforceable. Soon after the shootings at Virginia Tech, an offensive video game called *V-Tech Massacre* was made available on the Internet. Had a mainstream game company developed and sold *V-Tech Massacre*, it would have earned an adult rating. The game, however, was never sold in stores but instead was offered free to whomever wanted to download it. Had a law restricting this game been on the books, authorities would have been hard-pressed to find its creator, let alone stop its distribution. Furthermore, enforcement is likely to be inconsistent. Restrictions on speech tend to be enforced against unpopular people and ideas. For example, the government had targeted the Pacifica Foundation, which was cited by the FCC for violating the Broadcast Decency Rule, on account of its left-wing views. Finally, if the purpose of regulation is to reduce violence, it makes no sense to limit that regulation to entertainment. The ACLU argues: "Sports and the news are at least as violent as fiction, from the fights that erupt during every televised hockey game, to the videotaped beating of Rodney King by the L.A. Police Department, shown over and over again on prime time TV. If we accept censorship of violence in the media, we will have to censor sports and news programs."[8]

Censorship does more harm than good.

In *Kendrick*, Judge Posner argued that young people must be allowed to form their own political views, on the basis of uncensored speech, before they reach voting age. He added that people are unlikely to become responsible citizens if they are raised in what he called an "intellectual bubble." Protecting young people from nonpolitical speech is harmful as well. Overly protective regulations tend to reduce, rather than enhance, their ability to handle sensitive topics such as sex. It can also breed undesirable behavior such as authoritarianism, conformity, and lack of tolerance for unpopular opinions. Some argue that young people who are exposed early to the realities of adult life are less likely to engage in high-risk behavior.

Regulation also might rob future generations of classic works of art. Virginia Postrel, the editor of the libertarian magazine *Reason*, explains: "You *can* ban Shakespeare. It happened. In 1642, the greatest period of English theater was ended by an act of Parliament. The milieu that had produced Shakespeare, and that continued to perform his plays, was destroyed. Those theaters were full of sex, violence, and special effects—and of poetry, ideas, and creative promise."[9] A more recent example was the Hollywood blacklists of suspected Communists during the 1950s. Author Herbert Foerstel explains:

> The immediate effects of the blacklisting and the pervasive fear that McCarthyism planted in Hollywood was a self-censorship that produced vapid pictures and a paucity of talent. It is no coincidence that the golden age of Hollywood came to an end during the McCarthy Era. Films with social content were seen as a "red flag" by anticommunist politicians, and they soon disappeared from Hollywood.[10]

The threat of regulation can be almost as damaging to entertainment as regulation itself. On a number of occasions, such threats led to the adoption of industry codes that stifled expression. Foerstel notes that the film industry started blacklisting people with leftist sympathies after Senator Joseph McCarthy started to investigate alleged Communist infiltration of Hollywood. During the McCarthy era, Congress also investigated the comic book industry for allegedly inciting young readers to commit crime. *Reason*'s Postrel wrote:

> When congressional pressure and anti-competitive opportunism created the Comics Code, declaring American comic books an inherently childish medium,

FROM THE BENCH

United States v. Stevens, 533 F.3d 218 (3d Cir. 2008)

In 1999, Congress passed a law, 18 U.S.C. §48, banning the creation, sale, or possession of a depiction of animal cruelty with the intention of distributing it in interstate commerce. The law applied to "any visual or auditory depiction . . . in which a living animal is intentionally maimed, mutilated, tortured, wounded, or killed" and which had no serious social value.

The law's main target was "crush videos," in which women wearing high heels torture animals. The sounds of the animals, which are in great pain, could be heard in the videos. Crush videos appeal to people with a very specific sexual fetish. Federal prosecutors, however, used the law for a different purpose—namely, to combat dogfighting, which is illegal but still takes place underground. The first prosecution targeted Robert Stevens, who was charged with selling videos of dogfights.

Stevens argued that the law violated his right to free speech. In *United States v. Stevens*, 10 of the 13 judges on the U.S. Court of Appeals for the Third Circuit agreed with him. Judge D. Brooks Smith wrote the court's opinion. Initially, Judge Smith noted that the last time the Supreme Court had recognized a new category of speech that was unprotected by the First Amendment was in 1982, when it decided *Ferber v. New York*. In *Ferber*, the Court upheld a law outlawing the distribution of pornography that was not legally obscene but depicted children in sexual situations. The justices upheld that law as a means of "drying up" the market for child pornography and stopping sexual exploitation of young people.

Judge Smith found several important differences between crush videos and child pornography. Preventing cruelty to animals was a less compelling government interest than preventing sexual exploitation of children. Unlike human beings, animals lacked the awareness that a "permanent record" of their abuse, in the form of photos or videos, had been created. Furthermore, in the case of dogfighting, shutting down commerce in videos was unlikely to dry up the market for fights themselves because the fights were supported by live audiences.

EC Comics was destroyed and its readers bereft. That was the short-term effect. The larger loss was in the stories untold, the techniques unexplored. We can infer something of its magnitude by looking at the development of graphic storytelling in Europe and Japan. But we can never know what might have been.[11]

Smith expressed his concern that laws like this could erode free speech. The primary danger was that they required the accused to prove his or her speech had social value rather than forcing the government to prove it lacked social value. He added that unless obscenity was an issue, "the First Amendment does not require speech to have serious value in order for it to fall under the First Amendment umbrella," and that there was a "great spectrum" between speech that was "utterly without social value" and speech that had "high value." He also concluded that the law in question was too broadly written: "If a person hunts or fishes out of season, films the activity, and sells it to an out-of-state party, it appears that the statute has been violated. Similarly, the same person could be prosecuted for selling a film which contains a depiction of a bullfight in Spain if bullfighting is illegal in the state in which this person sells the film." Furthermore, since cruelty to animals was illegal everywhere in the United States, Smith reasoned that the new law would give animals little added protection and that the benefit of that protection was outweighed by the harm resulting from restricting speech.

Judge Robert Cowen wrote a dissenting opinion, in which he argued that the government had a compelling interest in stopping cruelty to animals, which had been protected by law as far back as colonial times; and that the speech involved in Stevens's videos had little, if any, social value. (He also pointed out that producing a dogfighting video *required* the commission of a crime.) He also contended that Congress reasonably could have concluded that banning the distribution of dogfight videos would in fact dry up the market for the fights themselves. Finally, he observed, "The speech outlawed by the statute at issue shares the salient characteristics of the other recognized categories of unprotected speech, and thus falls within the heartland of speech that may be proscribed based on its content."

The U.S. Supreme Court decided to review the appeals court's decision and heard oral arguments in October 2009.

Finally, some believe that the very idea of censorship is a relic of the Victorian era, when lawmakers feared that young people, women, and even working-class men would be led astray by exposure to popular entertainment. Others say that it is based on outmoded religious beliefs. They note that modern obscenity laws are derived from colonial laws against blasphemy (the inappropriate use of God's name) and point out that religious groups have played—and still do play—a prominent role in suppressing entertainment. In his dissenting opinion in *Ginsberg*, Justice William O. Douglas argued that attempting to regulate what some considered "sinful" was a step back in time to the era of Anthony Comstock, who believed that humans had an inborn tendency toward wrongdoing largely held in check by the fear of hell and that pornography was one of Satan's traps for the unwary. Douglas also said that it was one thing for religious organizations to get involved in the debate over entertainment, but quite a different matter for the state to get involved as a censor.

Summary

Entertainment is speech protected by the First Amendment, and therefore the government bears a heavy burden of justifying laws that restrict it. Laws regulating violent entertainment enable government officials to overrule parents' decisions about what their children see and hear and deny young people access to material that might make them well-informed citizens. The enforcement of laws regulating speech tends to be uneven and unfair, assuming that such laws can be enforced at all. Regulation may do more harm than good by, for example, depriving the public of classic works of art or overprotecting young people, leaving them less able to deal with the complexities of adult life. Finally some believe that restrictions on speech reflect the lingering influence of outmoded beliefs.

Looking Ahead

In our legal system, courts resolve disputes by analogy to earlier cases. Legal standards developed in the context of traditional media are being applied to new media such as video games and the Internet. The ongoing controversy over violent entertainment pits two powerful opposing interests: the First Amendment right to free expression and society's long-standing interest in protecting young citizens. Those who want to regulate entertainment have had some success in the legislative branch but have suffered a series of defeats in the courts. Two acts of Congress intended to protect young people from harmful online content were found unconstitutional; and, as of late 2009, the courts have upheld every challenge to state laws regulating young players' access to violent video games. Although the debate over violent entertainment stands at an impasse, supporters of regulation intend to continue their fight.

What Does Science Tell Us?

According to Lawrence Kutner and Cheryl Olson, doing research into the causes of violence is like solving a jigsaw puzzle with some pieces missing. There are many ways of fitting the pieces together, each of which will produce a different picture. The opposing sides in the debate over violent entertainment have arranged the scientific evidence to suit their own needs. Supporters of regulation believe that scientists have found enough evidence to tie violent entertainment to actual violence. In 2000, some of America's most prestigious medical organizations concluded that scientific studies "point overwhelmingly" to the conclusion that media violence causes aggressive behavior in some children. In fact, many in the public health community believe that the scientific debate over violent entertainment is settled.

Opponents of regulation argue that a statistical correlation between violent entertainment and aggressive behavior is not the same as an actual cause-and-effect relationship. Columnist Maggie Cutler wrote:

> Several studies have shown that violent boys tend to watch more TV, choose more violent content, and get more enjoyment out of it. But the studies admittedly can't show exactly how or why that happens. Do temperamentally violent kids seek out shows that express feelings they already have, or are they in it for the adrenaline boost? Do the sort of parents who let kids pig out on gore tend to do more than their share of other hurtful things that encourage violent behavior?[1]

Even though opponents insist that researchers have yet to rule out factors other than violent entertainment, this might not present an insurmountable barrier to regulation. Professor John Murray, a child psychologist at Kansas State University, says: "At some point, you have to say that if exposure to violence is related to aggressive attitudes and values, and if [the latter] are related to shooting classmates or acting aggressively—all of which we know to be true—then it stands to reason that there is probably a link between exposure to violence and aggressive actions."[2]

Are Courts Misapplying the First Amendment?

Supporters of regulation believe that the strict-scrutiny standard has prevented lawmakers from protecting young people from violent entertainment. Professor Kevin W. Saunders, a critic of that standard, accuses the courts of ignoring the *costs* of free expression. He also believes that judges do not understand how violent entertainment harms young people:

> No one suggests that a single exposure of a normal child to a film, video game, or CD will lead to immediate criminal behavior or permanent psychological injury. It is the continued exposure over the child's formative years that does harm. First Amendment theory has been incapable of handling such influences, and strict scrutiny is unlikely to be met.[3]

Saunders believes that the courts should adopt a "two-tier" approach to the First Amendment, under which laws aimed at protecting young people are judged on the less-restrictive rational-basis standard. Under this standard, which the Supreme Court used in *Ginsberg v. New York*, courts would find the scientific evidence strong enough to justify a broad range of regulations aimed at limiting young peoples' exposure to harmful entertainment.

Others view strict scrutiny as a needed check against the tendency to pass laws in the heat of the moment. After the mass shootings at Columbine, lawmakers considered bills that targeted the entertainment industry. Barbara Dority, the executive director of the Washington Coalition Against Censorship, wrote:

[W]e don't know why the [Columbine] murderers did what they did. We don't know why other incidents of school violence have occurred. We don't know if any one

The American Academy of Pediatrics' Recommendations

In 2001, the American Academy of Pediatrics (AAP) issued a statement on media violence, which summarized the effects of violent entertainment on young people and offered a series of recommendations. The following is adapted from the AAP's recommendations:

1. Pediatricians should incorporate a "media history" into young people's annual checkups and suggest healthy alternatives, such as sports, interactive play, and reading, for patients who are at risk. If the patient is a heavy user of media, the pediatrician should evaluate him or her for aggressive behavior, fears, or sleep disturbances, and intervene appropriately.

2. Pediatricians should encourage parents to limit their children's media consumption to one to two hours a day; use the V-chip; keep violent video games out of the sight of young children; and keep their children's bedrooms media-free.

3. Pediatricians should keep violent media out of hospitals and doctors' waiting rooms.

4. Pediatricians should encourage schools to teach media literacy as a way of protecting young people from the negative effects of exposure to violent media. "Media education involves teaching how media work, how media can influence the ways that we perceive reality and develop attitudes, how to determine whether media messages are appropriate, and how to reject messages that are not healthy."

5. Pediatricians should work within the health professions and with policy makers to keep media violence on the public health agenda. Experts in public health, psychology, and communications should focus future research efforts on ways to lessen the harmful effects of exposure to violent media.

6. Pediatricians should advocate for more "child-positive" media, not censorship. The pediatric community offers the following recommendations to the entertainment industry:

incident is meaningfully related to any other, or which
incidents, if any, are related to which of a variety of factors in our society.... As we await further information

- Avoid glamorizing weapon carrying and the normalization of violence as an acceptable way to resolve conflicts.

- Stop using violence in a comic or sexual context, or in a situation in which the violence is amusing, titillating, or trivialized.

- Eliminate portrayals of interpersonal violence and hateful, racist, misogynistic, or homophobic language or situations unless the portrayals explicitly show how destructive those words and actions can be.

- If violence is used, it should be used thoughtfully as serious drama, always showing the hurt and loss suffered by victims and perpetrators.

- Song lyrics should be made readily available to parents.

- Video games should not use human beings or other living things as targets or award points for killing.

- Violent video games should be restricted to age-limited areas of gaming arcades, and the distribution of violent video games or movies should be limited to appropriate age groups.

7. Pediatricians should advocate for simplified content-based media ratings that describe media content in several areas (such as violence, language, sex, or nudity). Content-descriptive ratings should be consistent across all entertainment media. "Just as it is important that parents know the ingredients in food they may feed to their children, they should be fully informed about the content of the media their children may use."

8. Pediatricians should remind their patients' families that, if they refuse to buy or use entertainment media that harm young people, these media will no longer be produced.

Source: American Academy of Pediatrics, Committee on Public Education. "Statement on Media Violence." *Pediatrics*, vol. 108, no. 5, pp. 1222–1226 (November 2001).

from law enforcement officials, it is our task—indeed, our duty as citizens—to resist panicked responses and stand in opposition to such tragedies being used to rationalize draconian violations of young peoples' civil liberties.[4]

Without strong First Amendment protection, young peoples' access to entertainment, and even their right to express themselves, might be curtailed in an effort to prevent another

The Experts' Findings About Media Violence

The following are excerpts from various government reports and studies pertaining to depictions of violence in the media:

National Commission on the Causes and Prevention of Violence, 1969
"While the evidence is incomplete, we can also assert the probability that mass media portrayals of violence are one major contributory factor which must be considered in attempts to explain the many forms of violent behavior that mark American society today."*

Surgeon General's Scientific Advisory Committee on Television and Social Behavior, 1972
"[The evidence supports] a preliminary and tentative indication of a causal relation between viewing violence on television and aggressive behavior" for "some children [who are predisposed to be aggressive] . . . in some environmental contexts."†

American Medical Association, 1976
The AMA's House of Delegates declares that "TV violence threatens the health and welfare of young Americans, commits itself to remedial actions with interested parties, and encourages opposition to TV programs containing violence and to their sponsors."‡

National Institute of Mental Health, 1982
"The consensus among most of the research community is that violence on television does lead to aggressive behavior by children and teenagers. . . . Not all children become aggressive, of course, but the correlations between

Columbine. Furthermore, a low standard of review would make it difficult for courts to distinguish restrictions based on scientific evidence from those based on emotion or prejudice.

Efforts to Regulate Violent Entertainment
Numerous bills that would restrict young peoples' access to violent entertainment have been debated in Congress. Some of those bills aimed to extend the harmful-to-minors doctrine and the Broadcast

violence and aggression are positive. In magnitude, television violence is as strongly correlated with aggressive behavior as any other behavioral variable that has been measured."§

American Psychological Association, 1993
"There is absolutely no doubt that higher levels of viewing violence on television are correlated with increased acceptance of aggressive attitudes and increased aggressive behavior."#

Joint Statement of the Public Health Community, 2000
"At this time, well over 1,000 studies point overwhelmingly to a causal connection between media violence and aggressive behavior in some children."¶

* Robert K. Baker and Sandra J. Ball, *Mass Media And Violence: A Report To The National Commission On The Causes And Prevention Of Violence*. Washington, D.C.: U.S. Government Printing Office, 1969, p. 375.
† Surgeon General's Scientific Advisory Committee on Television and Social Behavior, *Television and Growing Up: The Impact of Televised Violence*. Rockville, Md.: U.S. Public Health Service, Office of the Surgeon General, 1972, p. 11.
‡ American Medical Association. *Proceedings of the House of Delegates, June-July, 1976*. Chicago: 1976, p. 280.
§ National Institute of Mental Health. *Television and Behavior. Ten Years of Scientific Progress and Implications for the Eighties*. Rockville, Md.: U.S. Department of Health and Human Services, 1982, p. 6.
#American Psychological Association. *Violence and Youth: Psychology's Response: Volume 1: Summary Report of the American Psychological Association Commission on Violence and Youth*. Washington, D.C., 1993, p. 33.
¶ American Academy of Pediatrics. *Joint Statement on the Impact of Entertainment Violence on Children, Congressional Public Health Summit*, July 26, 2000. http://www.aap.org/advocacy/releases/jstmtEVC.htm.

Decency Rule to violent entertainment. They did not pass, largely because the federal courts had already expressed their reluctance to uphold such laws. This debate, however, is not over. Recently, the Federal Communications Commission (FCC) concluded that a rule banning violent television during hours when children were likely to be watching could survive a court challenge.

Congress has considered other bills aimed at violent entertainment. One proposal would specifically make the marketing of adult-rated content to underage audiences a deceptive trade practice. Supporters argue that industry self-regulation has been ineffective and that the government should be given the legal tools to punish offending companies and order them to change their marketing strategies. Opponents counter that the legislation could result in federal officials, not parents, deciding what entertainment is suitable for their children and that it could raise constitutional problems by giving industry ratings the force of law. Another bill would require entertainment companies to place labels advising buyers of possible psychological harm to young people on the packaging of violent content. Supporters argue that violent entertainment is a dangerous product, and therefore this requirement is no different from laws requiring health warnings on cigarette packages. Opponents, however, insist that the evidence offered to show that violent entertainment is harmful is much less conclusive than that linking smoking to cancer.

Some believe that Congress should revisit the issue of regulating harmful online content. Professor Saunders points out that underage customers are not allowed in adult bookstores, yet they are exposed to similar kinds of material on the Internet. That said, it is difficult to enforce age limits online. In fact, the problem of verifying ages was one reason why the Supreme Court found the Communications Decency Act (CDA) unconstitutional. Saunders proposes an alternative approach: a federal law requiring manufacturers of Internet software to make their products compatible with the Platform for Internet Content

Selection (PICS) system. Such a requirement is similar to laws requiring television sets to have a V-chip and requiring television programs to carry ratings. Saunders also supports requiring those posting adult-rated content to "tag" it so that Internet filters could block it. He calls such a requirement "a minor restriction on expression rights, more than justified by the interests parents have in determining the influences their children will experience as they grow into an adult world that has more robust expression rights."[5] The American Civil Liberties Union, however, considers mandatory ratings dangerous:

> People who disseminate quirky and idiosyncratic speech, create individual home pages, or post to controversial news groups, will be among the first Internet users blocked by filters and made invisible by the search engines. Controversial speech will still exist, but will only be visible to those with the tools and know-how to penetrate the dense smokescreen of industry "self-regulation."[6]

Alternatives to Regulation

There are various ways to reduce young peoples' exposure to violent entertainment that do not intrude on the First Amendment. Some legal approaches do not involve regulating content, including one proposal that involves amending the restraint-of-trade laws to allow the entertainment industry to enforce codes of conduct without fear of being sued. Such legislation would have the broadcasting industry readopt the 1952 Television Code, which committed the industry to maintaining high standards of programming, especially for young audiences. Another proposal would require cable companies to offer channels on an "a la carte" basis, thus allowing subscribers to reject channels they consider offensive. Yet another proposal would re-establish limits on the number of outlets a media company may own. Many critics believe that the recent waves of media consolidation that have concentrated outlets in the hands of a few companies are to blame for the low quality of entertainment.

Failed Federal Legislation Relating to Violent Entertainment

Violent entertainment has been a concern of Congress since the 1950s. Here are some recent examples of legislation that was introduced but did not become law:

S. 470, 104th Congress, The Children's Protection From Violent Programming Act of 1995

This bill would have extended the Broadcast Decency Rule to "violent video programming," with the Federal Communications Commission (FCC) having discretion to specify the hours during which violence would be restricted. Noncompliance with the rule would have been grounds for not renewing a broadcaster's license, and repeated noncompliance would have been grounds for revoking a license. News programs, documentaries, and sporting events would have been exempt from the rule if the FCC believed that those programs would not subject young viewers to the negative influences of televised violence.

H.R. 2036, 106th Congress, The Children's Defense Act of 1999

This bill—a criminal provision that applied to all entertainment media—was introduced soon after the Columbine shootings. Had the bill passed, a person found guilty of knowingly distributing explicit sexual or violent material to a person younger than 17 could have been imprisoned for up to five years. The bill also would have required retailers to make available the lyrics to recorded music they sold and would have granted the entertainment industry an antitrust exemption under which it could draw up and enforce guidelines regulating the sale of adult-rated materials.

S. 792, 107th Congress, The Media Marketing Accountability Act of 2001

This bill was a reaction to the Federal Trade Commission's finding that entertainment companies marketed violent entertainment to young audiences and

Both supporters and opponents of regulation agree on the need for media literacy training for young people, which is part of the curriculum in many Western countries. The American Psychological Association has stated:

that retailers were not enforcing the industry's age restrictions. This bill specifically defined marketing adult-rated entertainment to underage consumers as a deceptive trade practice. It also provided that a company's marketing practices would not be considered deceptive if it took part in an industry self-regulatory program that included penalties for noncompliance.

S. 616, 109th Congress, The Indecent and Gratuitous and Excessively Violent Programming Control Act

This bill addressed shortcomings in the broadcasting industry's rating system and the inability of the V-chip to prevent young viewers from watching violent programs. One provision would direct the FCC to assess current ratings and technology. If the FCC concluded that they were inadequate, it would be directed to adopt a rule "channeling" violent programs into the hours when young viewers are not reasonably likely to make up a substantial portion of the audience. Other provisions of the bill would require broadcasters and cable companies to provide clearer warnings about language, sexual content, and violence; obligate television stations to air programs designed to serve children's educational and informational needs; and encourage the broadcasting industry to reinstate the 1952 Television Code by exempting it from federal antitrust laws.

S. 2126, 109th Congress, The Family Entertainment Protection Act

This bill, aimed at the sale of adult-rated video games, would have made it a civil infraction to sell or rent to a person younger than 17 any video game rated "Mature," "Adults-Only," or "Ratings Pending" by the Entertainment Software Rating Board (ESRB). It also would have authorized the Federal Trade Commission (FTC) to evaluate the ESRB's rating system to guard against ratings "slippage"; conduct secret audits of businesses to find out how often underage customers were able to buy adult-rated video games; and determine whether "embedded content," such as the pornographic scenes inserted into the game *Grand Theft Auto: San Andreas*, was a widespread problem.

[T]he data dealing with media literacy curricula demonstrate that when children are taught how to view television critically, there is a reduction of TV viewing in general, and a clearer understanding of the messages conveyed by the medium. Studies on media literacy demonstrate when children are taught how to view television critically, children can feel less frightened and sad after discussions about the medium, can learn to differentiate between fantasy and reality, and can identify less with aggressive characters on TV, and better understand commercial messages.[7]

Some believe that American parents already have a technological tool that allows them to control their children's entertainment—the V-chip. A government-sponsored education program could increase parents' use of the chip. There are other tools as well. Jonathan Adelstein, a member of the FCC, explains:

Cable subscribers, for example, have various options available ... Digital cable set-top boxes allow parents to block shows with certain ratings, titles, or by time or date, and analog cable subscribers can use their set-top or "lockbox" technology that locks specific channels so that channel can no longer be viewed. Digital and personal video recorders, and video-on-demand permit families to "time-shift" or watch programming whenever they deem appropriate. Similarly, satellite TV subscribers have access to the Locks & Limits feature on DirecTV and Adult Guard on Dish Network.[8]

Finally, some favor wider use of independent ratings of entertainment. Deborah Taylor Tate, a member of the FCC, identified sources from outside the entertainment industry that have introduced new tools designed to help parents. For example, the Parents Television Council tracks every instance of violence, coarse language, sexual scenes, and suggestive dialogue on network programs; Common Sense Media has rated more than 6,000 media titles from a "kids and family" perspective and makes its ratings available to cable companies; and TV Guardian detects and filters out profanity and other offensive phrases chosen by the parent. Some independent organizations review and rate content and often offer more guidance than the entertainment industry's ratings. Independent ratings also reflect a diversity of religious and cultural beliefs and are consistent with free-market principles: Parents can choose from among various rating systems or simply make their own decisions.

Critics of this approach warn that private ratings could be as dangerous as outright government regulation. Author Marjorie Heins observes:

> Private rating companies ... treat their technologies as proprietary business information, and have only discretionary procedures for resolving complaints that sites have been wrongfully blocked. The cycle is completed when government agencies begin to rely upon or even mandate the use of private, unregulated rating and blocking systems, all in the interest of protecting youth.[9]

Furthermore, human raters are fallible or outright biased. In a controversy over requiring Internet filters in schools, researchers in Oregon discovered that some companies that sold filtering software had ties to conservative religious organizations, and some company representatives reportedly told school officials that their filtering criteria were consistent with conservative religious values.

Changing Attitudes and New Media

There are signs that Americans are becoming more aware that violent entertainment is unhealthy for their children. Some see a parallel to the portrayal of smoking. Forty years ago, television promoted smoking to Americans, through advertisements (banned since January 1, 1971) and on programs (something that by and large does not occur now). Professor Joanne Cantor says: "If public attitudes toward children's unfettered access to media violence can move in the direction of attitudes toward smoking or driving without a seatbelt, we will have made huge strides toward raising a healthier generation of young people."[10] Advocates note that the entertainment industry has reacted to changing attitudes toward racial and gender stereotypes and that it is only a matter of time before graphic violence falls out of favor as well.

Some believe that the entertainment of the future will cause even more serious harm than today's video games. Already, role-playing games such as *Second Life* allow users to create a virtual alter ego. Tomorrow's virtual games could enable players to experience a full range of human activity, including deeply taboo subjects such as rape, incest, and serial killing. In 2005, the American Psychological Association warned: "With the development of more sophisticated interactive media, such as virtual reality, the implications for violent content are of further concern, due to the intensification of more realistic experiences, and may also be more conducive to increasing aggressive behavior than passively watching violence on TV and in films."[11] But not everyone is pessimistic. Lawrence Kutner and Cheryl K. Olson say: "While concerns about the effects of violent video games are understandable, they're basically no different from the unfounded concerns previous generations had about the new media of their day. Remember, we're a remarkably resilient species."[12]

Professor Harold Schechter, who finds many parallels between today's violent entertainment and that of the past, urges us to keep the debate in perspective. He believes that future generations will find today's controversy over video games as amusing as we find the controversies about comic books in the 1950s. Schechter also says: "From the vantage point of the present—when the latest state-of-the-art entertainments seem to offer unprecedented levels of stimulation and lifelike gore—yesterday's popular culture always seems innocent and quaint."[13]

Summary

Supporters of regulation insist there is overwhelming evidence that violent entertainment is harmful and favor extending the Broadcast Decency Rule and the harmful-to-minors doctrine to violent material, along with restrictions on the way entertainment is marketed. Pro-regulation forces also accuse the courts of ignoring the social costs of giving broad First Amendment protection to harmful entertainment. Opponents of regulation counter that studies have failed to prove that violent entertainment causes real-world violence and add that some regulations are motivated by emotion and prejudice. They propose non-regulatory measures, ranging from parental-control technology to teaching media literacy to young people. Some believe that entertainment of the future could be even more harmful. Others insist that we humans will adapt to it, just as we have with existing forms of entertainment.

Beginning Legal Research

The goals of each book in the POINT/COUNTERPOINT series are not only to give the reader a basic introduction to a controversial issue affecting society, but also to encourage the reader to explore the issue more fully. This Appendix is meant to serve as a guide to the reader in researching the current state of the law as well as exploring some of the public policy arguments as to why existing laws should be changed or new laws are needed.

Although some sources of law can be found primarily in law libraries, legal research has become much faster and more accessible with the advent of the Internet. This Appendix discusses some of the best starting points for free access to laws and court decisions, but surfing the Web will uncover endless additional sources of information. Before you can research the law, however, you must have a basic understanding of the American legal system.

The most important source of law in the United States is the Constitution. Originally enacted in 1787, the Constitution outlines the structure of our federal government, as well as setting limits on the types of laws that the federal government and state governments can enact. Through the centuries, a number of amendments have added to or changed the Constitution, most notably the first 10 amendments, which collectively are known as the "Bill of Rights" and which guarantee important civil liberties.

Reading the plain text of the Constitution provides little information. For example, the Constitution prohibits "unreasonable searches and seizures" by the police. To understand concepts in the Constitution, it is necessary to look to the decisions of the U.S. Supreme Court, which has the ultimate authority in interpreting the meaning of the Constitution. For example, the U.S. Supreme Court's 2001 decision in *Kyllo v. United States* held that scanning the outside of a person's house using a heat sensor to determine whether the person is growing marijuana is an unreasonable search—if it is done without first getting a search warrant from a judge. Each state also has its own constitution and a supreme court that is the ultimate authority on its meaning.

Also important are the written laws, or "statutes," passed by the U.S. Congress and the individual state legislatures. As with constitutional provisions, the U.S. Supreme Court and the state supreme courts are the ultimate authorities in interpreting the meaning of federal and state laws, respectively. However, the U.S. Supreme Court might find that a state law violates the U.S. Constitution, and a state supreme court might find that a state law violates either the state or U.S. Constitution.

Not every controversy reaches either the U.S. Supreme Court or the state supreme courts, however. Therefore, the decisions of other courts are also important. Trial courts hear evidence from both sides and make a decision, while appeals courts review the decisions made by trial courts. Sometimes rulings from appeals courts are appealed further to the U.S. Supreme Court or the state supreme courts.

Lawyers and courts refer to statutes and court decisions through a formal system of citations. Use of these citations reveals which court made the decision or which legislature passed the statute, and allows one to quickly locate the statute or court case online or in a law library. For example, the Supreme Court case *Brown v. Board of Education* has the legal citation 347 U.S. 483 (1954). At a law library, this 1954 decision can be found on page 483 of volume 347 of the U.S. Reports, which are the official collection of the Supreme Court's decisions. On the following page, you will find samples of all the major kinds of legal citation.

Finding sources of legal information on the Internet is relatively simple thanks to "portal" sites such as findlaw.com and lexisone.com, which allow the user to access a variety of constitutions, statutes, court opinions, law review articles, news articles, and other useful sources of information. For example, findlaw.com offers access to all Supreme Court decisions since 1893. Other useful sources of information include gpo.gov, which contains a complete copy of the U.S. Code, and thomas.loc.gov, which offers access to bills pending before Congress, as well as recently passed laws. Of course, the Internet changes every second of every day, so it is best to do some independent searching.

Of course, many people still do their research at law libraries, some of which are open to the public. For example, some state governments and universities offer the public access to their law collections. Law librarians can be of great assistance, as even experienced attorneys need help with legal research from time to time.

Common Citation Forms

Source of Law	Sample Citation	Notes
U.S. Supreme Court	*Employment Division v. Smith*, 485 U.S. 660 (1988)	The U.S. Reports is the official record of Supreme Court decisions. There is also an unofficial Supreme Court ("S. Ct.") reporter.
U.S. Court of Appeals	*United States v. Lambert*, 695 F.2d 536 (11th Cir.1983)	Appellate cases appear in the Federal Reporter, designated by "F." The 11th Circuit has jurisdiction in Alabama, Florida, and Georgia.
U.S. District Court	*Carillon Importers, Ltd. v. Frank Pesce Group, Inc.*, 913 F.Supp. 1559 (S.D.Fla.1996)	Federal trial-level decisions are reported in the Federal Supplement ("F. Supp."). Some states have multiple federal districts; this case originated in the Southern District of Florida.
U.S. Code	Thomas Jefferson Commemoration Commission Act, 36 U.S.C., §149 (2002)	Sometimes the popular names of legislation—names with which the public may be familiar—are included with the U.S. Code citation.
State Supreme Court	*Sterling v. Cupp*, 290 Ore. 611, 614, 625 P.2d 123, 126 (1981)	The Oregon Supreme Court decision is reported in both the state's reporter and the Pacific regional reporter.
State Statute	Pennsylvania Abortion Control Act of 1982, 18 Pa. Cons. Stat. 3203-3220 (1990)	States use many different citation formats for their statutes.

Cases

Chaplinsky v. New Hampshire, 315 U.S. 568 (1942)

The U.S. Supreme Court held that "fighting words"—words likely to provoke the listener to retaliate—were not protected by the First Amendment. The Court said that fighting words had so little social value that any benefit that may be derived from them was clearly outweighed by society's interest in keeping order.

Winters v. New York, 333 U.S. 507 (1948) **and** *Joseph Burstyn, Inc. v. Wilson,* 343 U.S. 495 (1952)

In these two cases, the U.S. Supreme Court made it clear that entertainment was protected speech. The federal courts have extended the reasoning of *Burstyn* to new media such as the Internet and video games.

Ginsberg v. New York, 390 U.S. 629 (1968)

The U.S. Supreme Court concluded that "harmful-to-minors" laws were constitutional. Harmful-to-minors laws establish an age limit for soft-core pornography that is not obscene but because of its content is considered damaging to younger people. Some advocates argue that the harmful-to-minors doctrine should be extended to graphic violence.

Brandenburg v. Ohio, 395 U.S. 444 (1969)

The U.S. Supreme Court ruled that the First Amendment protected provocative language unless that language was "directed to inciting or producing imminent lawless action and is likely to incite or produce such action."

Miller v. California, 413 U.S. 15 (1973)

In this case, the U.S. Supreme Court announced a three-part test for what is obscene. The *Miller* test, which remains the law today, was an effort to accommodate local differences about what is acceptable and at the same time protect material with serious social value. *Miller* did not overrule *Ginsberg,* but it forced legislators to rewrite harmful-to-minors laws to incorporate the three *Miller* criteria.

Sable Communications of California, Inc. v. Federal Communications Commission, 492 U.S. 115 (1989)

Today, the U.S. Supreme Court applies a "strict-scrutiny" standard to laws that regulate the content of speech. That standard was spelled out in this key case, which requires that the government establish a compelling interest in regulating speech and that the law in question be the least-restrictive way of furthering that interest.

Miramax Films Corporation v. Motion Picture Association of America, Inc., 148 Misc. 2d 1, 560 N.Y.S.2d 730 (N.Y. Sup. Ct., New York County 1990)

In this case, a film studio challenged the film industry's decision to give a film an X (adults only) rating on account of its sexual content. Although the judge found no legal basis to overturn the rating, he criticized the industry's rating system for failing to account for the harmful effects of on-screen violence on young moviegoers.

133

Eclipse Enterprises, Inc. v. Gulotta, 134 F.3d 63 (2d Cir. 1997)
A federal appeals court overturned a county ordinance banning the sale of "true crime" trading cards to young people. It rejected the notion that violence could be regulated along the same lines as pornography and found the county's definition of violence overly broad.

Reno v. American Civil Liberties Union, 521 U.S. 344 (1997)
The U.S. Supreme Court struck down those portions of the Communications Decency Act (CDA) that required people who posted Internet content that was "indecent" or "patently offensive" to prevent users younger than 17 from accessing it. After the CDA was overturned, Congress passed a narrower law, the Child Online Protection Act (COPA), which was aimed at material deemed "harmful to minors." That law was also found unconstitutional.

American Amusement Machine Association v. Kendrick, 244 F.3d 572 (7th Cir. 2001)
The appeals court concluded that video games were protected by the First Amendment and found that the scientific evidence of the games' harmfulness was not conclusive enough to justify regulating them. Since then, every appeals court decision dealing with video game regulation has reached the same result. The most recent decision was *Video Software Dealers Association v. Schwarzenegger*, No. 07-16620 (U.S. Ct. App., 9th Cir., Feb. 20, 2009). In that case, the court also ruled that the harmful-to-minors doctrine was limited to pornography and could not be extended to violence.

James v. Meow Media, Inc., 300 F.3d 683 (6th Cir. 2002)
This was a lawsuit filed by the victims of a school shooting against the entertainment companies whose products allegedly influenced the teenage shooter. A federal appeals court concluded that violent entertainment was not covered by product liability laws and that the shooter's actions, not the entertainment he chose, was the legal cause of the victims' deaths.

United States v. Stevens, 533 F.3d 218 (3d Cir. 2008)
This case overturned a federal law that banned trafficking in video depictions of cruelty to animals. The majority concluded that the government's interest in protecting animals was not strong enough to justify creating a new category of speech that was outside the protection of the First Amendment.

Statutes
Broadcast Decency Rule, 47 C.F.R. §73.399
Radio and television broadcasts have a lower level of First Amendment protection than other media. Broadcasters must follow the rules of the Federal Communications Commission (FCC). Those rules include the Broadcast Decency Rule, which limits indecent programming to the hours between 10 P.M. and 6 A.M., when young people are less likely to be in the audience. The rule applies to material dealing with sexual activity or excretory functions. The FCC recently said, however, that the rule should be extended to violence. Other advocates believe that the rule should be extended to non-broadcast media as well.

Terms and Concepts

Age-based ratings
Aggressiveness
Broadcast Decency Rule
Catharsis
Causation
Censorship
Commercial speech
Compelling interest
Correlational study
Deceptive trade practices
Desensitization
Entertainment Software Rating Board (ESRB)
Federal Communications Commission (FCC)
Federal Trade Commission (FTC)
First Amendment
First-person games
Harmful to minors
Indecency
Interactive media
Hicklin doctrine
Least-restrictive means
Longitudinal study
Media literacy
Miller obscenity test
Minors
Motion Picture Association of America (MPAA)
National Association of Broadcasters (NAB)
Obscenity
Parental Advisory
Rational-basis test
Recording Industry Association of America (RIAA)
Self-regulation
Strict scrutiny
Television Code of 1952
Universal ratings
V-chip
X rating

Introduction: Violence, Entertainment, and Society

1 Craig A. Anderson and Karen E. Dill, "Video Games and Aggressive Thoughts, Feelings, and Behavior in the Laboratory and in Life," *Journal of Personality and Social Psychology* 78, no. 4 (2000): p. 772.
2 Hillary Rodham Clinton, quoted in Paul Keegan, "Culture Quake," *Mother Jones,* November/December 1999.
3 U.S. Constitution, First Amendment.
4 *Mutual Film Corporation v. Industrial Commission of Ohio,* 236 U.S. 230, 244 (1915).
5 *Winters v. New York,* 333 U.S. 507, 510 (1948).
6 *Joseph Burstyn, Inc. v. Wilson,* 343 U.S. 495, 501 (1952).
7 N.Y. Penal Law §1141(2), which was found unconstitutional in *Winters v. New York,* 1948.
8 *Miller v. California,* 413 U.S. 15, 24 (1973).
9 *Enforcement of Prohibitions Against Broadcast Indecency in 18 U.S.C. §1864,* F.C.C. Record, vol. 8, p. 705 (1993).
10 Lawrence Kutner and Cheryl K. Olson, *Grand Theft Childhood: The Surprising Truth About Violent Video Games and What Parents Can Do.* New York: Simon & Schuster, 2008, p. 45.
11 Fredric Wertham, quoted in Ibid., p. 51.
12 Brandon S. Centerwall, "Special Communication: Television and Violence: The Scale of the Problem and Where to Go from Here," *Journal of the American Medical Association* 267, no. 22 (June 10, 1992).
13 American Academy of Pediatrics. "Joint Statement on the Impact of Entertainment Violence on Children," Congressional Public Health Summit, July 26, 2000. http://www.aap.org/advocacy/releases/jstmtEVC.htm.
14 Testimony of Donald E. Cook, M.D., president of the American Academy of Pediatrics, before the U.S. Senate Commerce Committee, September 13, 2000. http://www.aap.org/advocacy/releases/mediaviolencetestimony.pdf.
15 *Sable Communications of California, Inc. v. Federal Communications Commission,* 492 U.S. 115, 126 (1989).

Point: Violent Entertainment Is a Serious Problem

1 Texas Execution Information Center, Ronald Howard. http://www.txexecutions.org/reports/350.asp.
2 American Academy of Pediatrics, Committee on Public Education. "Statement on Media Violence." *Pediatrics* 108, no. 5 (November 2001): p. 1224.
3 Kevin W. Saunders, *Saving Our Children from the First Amendment.* New York: New York University Press, 2003, p. 160.
4 American Academy of Pediatrics, Committee on Public Education. "Statement on Media Violence," p. 1223.
5 American Academy of Pediatrics. "Joint Statement on the Impact of Entertainment Violence on Children."
6 Brandon S. Centerwall, "Special Communication: Television and Violence: The Scale of the Problem and Where to Go from Here."
7 American Academy of Pediatrics, Committee on Public Education. "Statement on Media Violence," p. 1223.
8 Senate Committee on the Judiciary, "Children, Violence, and the Media: A Report for Parents and Policy Makers," September 14, 1999.
9 Ibid.
10 American Academy of Pediatrics, Committee on Public Education. "Statement on Media Violence," pp. 1223–1224.
11 Eugene Provenzo, quoted in Paul Keegan, "Culture Quake."

Counterpoint: The Dangers of Violent Entertainment Are Exaggerated

1 *Video Software Dealers Association v. Schwarzenegger,* 556 F.3d 950 (9th Cir. 2009).
2 Federal Communications Commission, *In the Matter of Violent Television Programming and Its Impact on Children,* No. FCC 07-50, April 25, 2007, p. 10.
3 Free Expression Policy Project. *Fact Sheets: Media Violence.* New York, 2004. http://www.fepproject.org/factsheets/mediaviolence.html.
4 *In the Matter of Violent Television Programming and Its Impact on Children,* p. 6.

5 Gerard Jones, quoted in Harold Schechter, *Savage Pastimes: A Cultural History of Violent Entertainment.* New York: St. Martin's Press, 2005, p. 152.
6 Benjamin Radford, "Reality Check on Video Game Violence," LiveScience.com, December 4, 2005. http://www.livescience.com/technology/051204_video_violence.html.
7 Maggie Cutler, "Whodunit—the Media?" *The Nation*, March 26, 2001.
8 *James v. Meow Media, Inc.*, 300 F.3d 683, 693 (6th Cir. 2002).
9 Richard Rhodes, "The Media Violence Myth." *Rolling Stone*, November 23, 2000.
10 Schechter, *Savage Pastimes*, p. 88.
11 Ibid., p. 111.

Point: The Entertainment Industry Has Acted Irresponsibly
1 Mary Lou Dickerson made those remarks on PBS's *The NewsHour with Jim Lehrer* on July 7, 2003. She is quoted in Lawrence Kutner and Cheryl K. Olson, *Grand Theft Childhood*, p. 8.
2 Newton N. Minow and Craig LaMay, *Abandoned in the Wasteland: Children, Television, and the First Amendment.* New York: Hill and Wang, 1995, p. 127.
3 Testimony of Donald E. Cook, M.D., president of the American Academy of Pediatrics, before the U.S. Senate Commerce Committee, September 13, 2000.
4 Tricia Rose. *The Hip Hop Wars: What We Talk About When We Talk About Hip Hop—and Why It Matters.* New York: Basic Books, 2008, p. 58.
5 Ibid., p. 197.
6 Federal Trade Commission. *Marketing Violent Entertainment to Children: A Review of Self-Regulation and Industry Practices in the Motion Picture, Music Recording & Electronic Game Industries.* Washington, D.C.: 2000, p. i.
7 Nicholas L. Carnagey, Craig A. Anderson, and Brad J. Bushman, "The Effect of Video Game Violence on Physiological Desensitization to Real-Life Violence," *Journal of Experimental Social Psychology* 43 (2007): p. 495.
8 Federal Communications Commission, *In the Matter of Violent Television Programming and Its Impact on Children*, pp. 15–16.
9 Testimony of Dale Kunkel before the Senate Committee on Government Affairs, July 25, 2001.
10 Saunders, *Saving Our Children from the First Amendment*, p. 7.
11 Symposium, "Should States Sue the Entertainment Industry as They Did Big Tobacco?" *Insight on the News*, October 30, 2000.

Counterpoint: Critics Wrongly Blame Entertainment for Crime
1 Kutner and Olson, *Grand Theft Childhood*, p. 159.
2 Schechter, *Savage Pastimes*, p. 9.
3 Rose, *The Hip Hop Wars*, p. 107.
4 Ibid., p. 51.
5 Federal Communications Commission, *In the Matter of Violent Television Programming and Its Impact on Children*, p. 26.
6 Schechter, *Savage Pastimes*, p. 156.
7 Rose, *The Hip Hop Wars*, p. 123.
8 Schechter, *Savage Pastimes*, pp. 119–120.
9 Kutner and Olson, *Grand Theft Childhood*, p. 34.
10 Gershon Legman, quoted in Schechter, *Savage Pastimes*, p. 15.
11 Schechter, *Savage Pastimes*, p. 157.
12 Gerard Jones, "Violent Media Is Good for Kids," *Mother Jones*, June 28, 2000.

Point: Regulating Entertainment Is Necessary
1 Press Release, "Morality in Media President's Statement on MPAA Decision to Stand By Its R-Rating for the Sadistic, Graphically Violent Film *Hostel*," Morality in Media Inc., March 30, 2006. http://www.moralityinmedia.org.
2 Kutner and Olson, *Grand Theft Childhood*, p. 171.
3 Gregg Easterbrook, "Watch and Learn," *The New Republic*, May 17, 1999.
4 *Ginsberg v. New York*, 390 U.S. 629, 642 (1968), fn. 10.
5 Federal Communications Commission, *In the Matter of Violent Television Programming and Its Impact on Children*, p. 12.
6 Saunders, *Saving Our Children from the First Amendment*, p. 90.

7 *Ginsberg v. New York*, 390 U.S. 629, 638 (1968), fn 6.

8 *Ginsberg v. New York*, 390 U.S. 629, 639 (1968).

9 Saunders, *Saving Our Children from the First Amendment*, p. 32.

10 *Ginsberg v. New York*, 390 U.S. 629, 641–643 (1968).

11 Saunders, *Saving Our Children from the First Amendment*, p. 65.

12 *Winters v. New York*, 333 U.S. 507, 534 (1948) (Frankfurter, J., dissenting).

Counterpoint: Regulating Entertainment Is Bad Policy

1 *American Amusement Machine Association v. Kendrick*, 244 F.3d 572, 578 (7th Cir. 2001).

2 *United States v. Stevens*, No. 05-2497 533 F.3d 218 (3d Circ. 2008).

3 *American Amusement Machine Association v. Kendrick*, 244 F.3d 572, 574 (7th Cir. 2001).

4 Testimony of Hilary Rosen before the U.S. Senate Commerce Committee, September 13, 2000.

5 *Action for Children's Television v. Federal Communications Commission*, 58 F.3d 654, 678 (D.C. Cir. 1995) (Edwards, J., dissenting).

6 *Interactive Digital Software Association v. St. Louis County*, 329 F.3d 954, 960 (8th Cir. 2002).

7 *In the Matter of Violent Television Programming and Its Impact on Children*, No. FCC 07-50 (Federal Communications Commission, April 25, 2007). p. 20.

8 American Civil Liberties Union. *Freedom of Expression in the Arts and Entertainment*. Briefing Paper Number 14. New York, 2002. http://www.aclu. org/freespeech/gen/11046res20020227. html.

9 Virginia Postrel, "Creative Matrix: What We Lose by Regulating Culture," *Reason*, August/September 1999.

10 Herbert N. Foerstel, *Banned in the Media: A Reference Guide to Censorship*

in the Press, Motion Pictures, Broadcasting, and the Internet. Westport, Conn.: Greenwood Press, 1998, p. 22.

11 Postrel, "Creative Matrix: What We Lose by Regulating Culture."

Conclusion: Looking Ahead

1 Cutler, "Whodunit—the Media?"

2 John Murray, quoted in Paul Keegan, "Culture Quake," *Mother Jones*, November/December 1999.

3 Saunders, *Saving Our Children from the First Amendment*, p. 258.

4 Barbara Dority, "The Columbine Tragedy: Countering the Hysteria," *The Humanist*, July 1999.

5 Saunders, *Saving Our Children from the First Amendment*, p. 178.

6 American Civil Liberties Union. *Fahrenheit 451.2: Is Cyberspace Burning?* New York: March 17, 2002. http://www.aclu.org/news/NewsPrint. cfm?ID=9997&c=252.

7 American Psychological Association. *Resolution on Violence in Video Games and Interactive Media*. Washington, D.C.: 2005. http://www.apa.org/releases/ resolutionvideoviolence.pdf.

8 Federal Communications Commission, *In the Matter of Violent Television Programming and Its Impact on Children*, p. 32 (Statement of Commissioner Jonathan S. Adelstein).

9 Marjorie Heins, *Not In Front of the Children: "Indecency," Censorship, and the Innocence of Youth*. New York: Hill and Wang, 2001, p. 165.

10 Joanne Cantor, "What We Can Do About Media Violence: Promoting Public Education and Parental Empowerment to Raise a Healthier Generation," *Wisconsin School News*, September 2000.

11 American Psychological Association, *Resolution on Violence in Video Games and Interactive Media*.

12 Kutner and Olson, *Grand Theft Childhood*, p. 229.

13 Schechter, *Savage Pastimes*, p. 18

Books

Foerstel, Herbert N. *Banned in the Media: A Reference Guide to Censorship in the Press, Motion Pictures, Broadcasting, and the Internet.* Westport, Conn.: Greenwood Press, 1998.

Heins, Marjorie. *Not In Front of the Children: "Indecency," Censorship, and the Innocence of Youth.* New York: Hill and Wang, 2001.

Kutner, Lawrence, and Cheryl K. Olson. *Grand Theft Childhood: The Surprising Truth About Violent Video Games and What Parents Can Do.* New York: Simon & Schuster, 2008.

Minow, Newton N., and Craig LaMay. *Abandoned in the Wasteland: Children, Television, and the First Amendment.* New York: Hill and Wang, 1995.

Rose, Tricia. *The Hip Hop Wars: What We Talk About When We Talk About Hip Hop—and Why It Matters.* New York: Basic Books, 2008.

Saunders, Kevin W. *Saving Our Children from the First Amendment.* New York: New York University Press, 2003.

Schechter, Harold. *Savage Pastimes: A Cultural History of Violent Entertainment.* New York: St. Martin's Press, 2005.

Reports

American Academy of Pediatrics. "Joint Statement on the Impact of Entertainment Violence on Children." Congressional Public Health Summit, July 26, 2000. Available online. URL: http://www.aap.org/advocacy/releases/jstmtEVC.htm.

American Civil Liberties Union. *Fahrenheit 451.2: Is Cyberspace Burning?* New York, March 17, 2002. Available online. URL: http://www.aclu.org/news/NewsPrint.cfm?ID=9997&c=252.

———. *Freedom of Expression in the Arts and Entertainment.* Briefing Paper Number 14. New York, 2002. Available online. URL: http://www.aclu.org/freespeech/gen/11046res20020227.html.

American Psychological Association. *Resolution on Violence in Video Games and Interactive Media.* Washington, D.C.: 2005. Available online. URL: http://www.apa.org/releases/resolutionvideoviolence.pdf.

RESOURCES ||||▷

Enforcement of Prohibitions Against Broadcast Indecency in 18 U.S.C. §1864, F.C.C. Record, vol. 8, p. 705 (1993).

Federal Communications Commission, *In the Matter of Violent Television Programming and Its Impact on Children,* No. FCC 07-50. April 25, 2007.

Federal Trade Commission. *Marketing Violent Entertainment to Children: A Review of Self-Regulation and Industry Practices in the Motion Picture, Music Recording & Electronic Game Industries.* Washington, D.C., 2000.

Free Expression Policy Project. *Fact Sheets: Media Violence.* New York, 2004. Available online. URL: http://www.fepproject.org/factsheets/mediaviolence.html.

Testimony of Dale Kunkel before the Senate Committee on Government Affairs, July 25, 2001.

Testimony of Donald E. Cook, M.D., president of the American Academy of Pediatrics, before the U.S. Senate Commerce Committee, September 13, 2000. Available online. URL: http://www.aap.org/advocacy/releases/mediaviolencetestimony.pdf.

Testimony of Hilary Rosen, before the U.S. Senate Commerce Committee, September 13, 2000.

Texas Execution Information Center, Ronald Howard. Available online. URL: http://www.txexecutions.org/reports/350.asp.

Articles

American Academy of Pediatrics, Committee on Public Education. "Statement on Media Violence." *Pediatrics* 108, no. 5 (November 2001).

Anderson, Craig A., and Karen E. Dill. "Video Games and Aggressive Thoughts, Feelings, and Behavior in the Laboratory and in Life." *Journal of Personality and Social Psychology* 78, no. 4 (2000).

Cantor, Joanne. "What We Can Do About Media Violence: Promoting Public Education and Parental Empowerment to Raise a Healthier Generation." *Wisconsin School News,* September 2000.

Carnagey, Nicholas L., Craig A. Anderson, and Brad J. Bushman. "The Effect of Video Game Violence on Physiological Desensitization to Real-Life Violence," *Journal of Experimental Social Psychology* 43 (2007).

Centerwall, Brandon S. "Special Communication: Television and Violence: The Scale of the Problem and Where to Go from Here." *Journal of the American Medical Association* 267, no. 22 (June 10, 1992).

Cutler, Maggie. "Whodunit—the Media?" *The Nation*, March 26, 2001.

Dority, Barbara. "The Columbine Tragedy: Countering the Hysteria." *The Humanist*, July 1999.

Easterbrook, Gregg. "Watch and Learn." *The New Republic*, May 17, 1999.

Jones, Gerard. "Violent Media Is Good for Kids." *Mother Jones*, June 28, 2000.

Keegan, Paul. "Culture Quake." *Mother Jones*, November/December 1999.

"Morality in Media President's Statement on MPAA Decision to Stand By Its R-Rating for the Sadistic, Graphically Violent Film *Hostel*." Morality in Media Inc., March 30, 2006. Available online. URL: http://www.moralityinmedia.org.

Postrel, Virginia. "Creative Matrix: What We Lose by Regulating Culture." *Reason*, August/September 1999.

Radford, Benjamin. "Reality Check on Video Game Violence." LiveScience.com, December 4, 2005. Available online. URL: http://www.livescience.com/technology/051204_video_violence.html.

Rhodes, Richard. "The Media Violence Myth." *Rolling Stone*, November 23, 2000.

Symposium. "Should States Sue the Entertainment Industry as They Did Big Tobacco?" *Insight on the News*, October 30, 2000.

Web Sites
American Civil Liberties Union
http://www.aclu.org
> The ACLU, the nation's oldest civil-liberties organization, has gone to court to stop Congress and the states from imposing restrictions on speech, including entertainment.

Federal Communications Commission
http://www.fcc.gov
> The FCC is responsible for licensing and regulating the broadcast industry and punishing violators of its rules, including the Broadcast Decency Rule.

RESOURCES ||||▷

Federal Trade Commission
http://www.ftc.gov
The FTC is responsible for enforcing laws that ban "unfair or deceptive trade practices," a broad category that includes deceptive advertising and marketing. The FTC also investigates industry practices that may be unfair or deceptive.

Free Expression Policy Project
http://www.fepproject.org
This organization seeks "free speech–friendly" solutions to the concerns that drive censorship campaigns.

Morality in Media, Inc.
http://www.moralityinmedia.org
This organization's main focus is on pornography, but it also opposes graphic depictions of violence.

Motion Picture Association of America
http://www.mpaa.org
In 1968, the Motion Picture Association of America created an age-based rating system that replaced the Hays Code. It has become the model for other industries' rating systems.

National Association of Broadcasters
http://www.nab.org
The National Association of Broadcasters began rating programs in 1997, when it introduced the TV Parental Guidelines, which may be found at http://www.tvguidelines.org.

National Coalition Against Censorship
http://www.ncac.org
This alliance of civil liberties, artistic, educational, and professional organizations opposes restrictions on speech, especially artistic expression.

Parents Television Council
http://www.parentstv.org
This organization advocates "positive, family-oriented television programming" and tough enforcement of the Broadcast Decency Rule.

Recording Industry Association of America
http://www.riaa.com
The Recording Industry Association of America has overseen a "Parental Advisory Label" program, under which individual record companies place warning stickers on packages of recordings containing explicit lyrics.

U.S. Department of Justice
http://www.usdoj.gov
The Justice Department enforces federal laws, including those banning obscenity.

PICTURE CREDITS

A

Action for Children's Television v. Federal Communications Commission, 89, 104–106
addiction, 38
Adelstein, Jonathan, 93, 126
African Americans, 57
African-American culture, 78
aggression vs. violence, 48
Almodovar, Pedro, 96
American Academy of Pediatrics (AAP)
  on evidence for link, 22, 33
  on glamorization of violence, 29
  recommendations of, 118–119
  on time spent using media, 27
  on video games, 38–39
American Amusement Machine Association v. Kendrick, 80–82, 90, 101, 102–103, 110–111
American Civil Liberties Union (ACLU), 107, 123
American Medical Association (AMA), 19, 120
American Psychological Association (APA), 47–48, 57, 121, 125–126, 128
Anderson, Craig A., 11–12, 38, 50–51, 61
anecdotal evidence, 47
animal cruelty, 112–113
antisocial behavior, encouragement of, 56–57

art, 111
attitudes, changing, 127–129
average American parent standard, 96–97

B

Beltway sniper, 54–55
bias, 42–43, 75–78, 127
blacklisting, 111
blaxploitation films, 57
Boggs, Danny, 51, 104–105
brain development, 92–93
Brandenburg, Charles, 59
Brandenburg v. Ohio, 59
Braveheart (film), 51–52
Brennan, William, 20–21, 88–89
Broadcast Decency Rule, 16, 78, 88–89, 91, 103–106, 124
Buckley, James, 89
Bully (video game), 57
Bush, George H.W., 77–78
Bushman, Brad J., 38, 61
Bushnell, Nolan, 55
Butler v. Michigan, 15

C

Callahan, Consuelo, 76–77
Cantor, Joanne, 128
Carlin, George, 88
Carnagey, Nicholas L., 61
Carneal, Michael, 29, 38, 51, 69, 104–105
catharsis theory, 37
causation
  correlation vs., 40–41, 49, 116
  inconclusivity, 43
  in law, 51
censorship, 18, 96, 107, 110–114

Centerwall, Brandon, 28, 32, 34–35
channeling of content to nighttime hours, 91, 92–93, 125
Chaplinsky, Walter, 58
Chaplinsky v. New Hampshire, 58, 87
Child Online Protection Act (COPA), 24, 45
child pornography, 112
child-positive media, 118–119
children. *See* minors
Children's Defense Act of 1999 (bill), 124
Children's Protection from Violent Programming Act of 1995 (bill), 124
Cho, Seung-Hui, 47, 83
cigarette marketing, 60
Clinton, Bill, 66
Clinton, Hillary Rodham, 12
Clockwork Orange (film), 55
coarse entertainment, increase in, 55–56
Columbia County Longitudinal Study (New York), 30–32
Columbine High School shootings, 11–12, 47, 117–118
comic books, 18, 112–113
Comics Code, 112–113
Common Sense Media, 127
Communications Decency Act (CDA), 24, 44, 122
community standards test, 45
Comstock, Anthony, 14, 107, 110, 114
Condon, Charlie, 68

content-descriptive rat-
ings, 119
Cook, Donald, 36–37, 56
correlation
causation vs., 40–41,
49, 116
between entertainment
violence and behavior,
33–34, 36–37
Cowen, Robert, 113
"creative violence," 84
crime, "true." *See* "true
crime" publications
crime rates
FBI on, 47
historical, 79, 82
juvenile, 44–46
television and, 34–35,
46
as unrelated to
availability of violent
entertainment, 44–46
criminal syndicalism
laws, 59
crush videos, 112–113
cultural bias, 78
Cutler, Maggie, 47–48,
116

D
death penalty, 52
desensitization to vio-
lence, 32–33, 36, 37,
56
Dickerson, Mary Lou, 54
Dill, Karen, 11–12
dime novels, 17
disrespect of others,
56–57
dogfighting, 112–113
Dority, Barbara, 117–120
Douglas, William O., 114
drugs, 72–73

E
Easterbrook, Gregg, 55,
87, 90

*Eclipse Enterprises, Inc. v.
Gulotta*, 72–73, 90
Edwards, Harry, 104–106
emotions, management
of, 83–84
enforceability of regula-
tions, 110
England, 79
*Entertainment Software
Association v. Blago-
jevich*, 51
*Entertainment Software
Association v. Gran-
holm*, 82, 109
Entertainment Software
Rating Board (ESRB),
21, 64
Eron, Leonard, 30, 31–32
EverQuest (video game),
70
exaggeration of impact
of violent entertain-
ment, 42–43
executions, depictions of,
51–52

F
Family Entertainment
Protection Act (bill),
125
Federal Communications
Commission (FCC)
authority to regulate, 88
Broadcast Decency Rule
and, 78, 88
complaints to, 103
regulation by, 16
report on television
violence, 92–93
*Federal Communications
Commission v. Pacifica
Foundation*, 16, 88–89
Federal Trade Commis-
sion (FTC), 43, 60,
66–67
Ferber v. New York, 112
field experiments, 41
"fighting words," 58, 87

First Amendment and
freedom of speech.
See also specific cases
animal cruelty and,
112–113
broadcast media, lower
level of protection for,
44, 88
criminal syndicalism
laws and, 59
entertainment as
protected speech,
102–103
"fighting words" and, 58
protections and limits
on free speech and
obscenity, 12–16, 17,
23–24, 44, 77
public support for, 90
rights of minors,
limited, 95–97
wording of, 12
Foerstel, Herbert, 111
Frankfurter, Felix, 23,
87, 99
Free Expression Policy
Project, 42–43
Freedman, Jonathan, 41
freedom of speech. *See*
First Amendment and
freedom of speech

G
Ginsberg, Sam, 20–21
Ginsberg v. New York,
15–16, 20–21, 76–77,
91, 95, 98, 114
glamorization of vio-
lence, 29, 119
glorification of violence,
20, 72, 75
Gore, Tipper, 20
Grand Guignol, 52
Grand Theft Auto (video
game), 75, 125
Grand Theft Childhood
(Kutner and Olson),
48

INDEX ///▷

The Great Train Robbery (film), 17–18
Griesa, Thomas, 73, 90
Grossman, Dave, 36–37

H
harmful-to-minors doctrine
in *American Amusement Machine Association v. Kendrick*, 80–82
Child Online Protection Act and, 45
in *Eclipse Enterprises, Inc. v. Gulotta*, 72–73
in *Ginsberg v. New York*, 20
judges troubled by, 106–107
Michigan law and, 109
in *Miller v. California*, 15–16
in *Video Software Dealers Association v. Schwarzeneger*, 76–77, 103
Harris, Eric, 11, 47
hate speech, 57
Hawkins, Gordon, 35
Hays Code, 18
heavy metal music, 36
Heins, Marjorie, 47, 127
Hicklin, The Queen v., 15, 106
hip-hop music, 57, 72–74, 78
history
crime rates in, 79, 82
of human violence, 71
homicide rates and television, 34–35
Hostel (film), 86–87
Howard, Ronald Ray, 26
Huesmann, L. Rowell, 30–31, 34–35
human nature as violent, 71

I
imitation of violence, 29, 34, 37, 46–47
Indecent and Gratuitous and Excessively Violent Programming Control Act (bill), 125
indecent material, 16, 24, 44, 88–89
independent ratings, 126–127
individual rights, infringement of, 103–107
Interactive Digital Software Association v. St. Louis County, 106
interactive media, 36, 81–82, 128. *See also* video games
Internet
enforcement difficulties, 122
First Amendment and, 44
as media reinforcement, 38
Platform for Internet Content Selection (PICS) system, 122–123
pornography on, 24
regulation of, 24, 44–45

J
Jackson, Janet, 89
James v. Meow Media, Inc., 51, 104–105
Jones, Sarah, 78
Joseph Burstyn, Inc. v. Wilson, 14, 102
juvenile crime rates, 44–46

K
Kaiser Family Foundation survey, 65–67, 83

King, Rodney, 110
Klebold, Dylan, 11, 47
Ku Klux Klan, 59
Kunkel, Dale, 65
Kutner, Lawrence, 18, 42, 48–49, 70, 83, 87, 128

L
laboratory experiments, 30–31, 41–42
lawsuits against entertainment industry, 68–69, 104–105
legal standards
"average American parent," 96–97
community standards test, 45
rational-basis, 21, 77, 98, 117
rational-relationship, 76
strict-scrutiny, 23–24, 45, 76, 98, 117
Legman, Gershon, 79, 82
liability lawsuits, 104–105
lockbox technology, 126
logic, faulty, 49
longitudinal studies, 30–31

M
Males, Michael, 41–42
Malvo, John Lee, 38, 54–55
marketing by entertainment industry
FTC report on, 60, 66–67
Media Marketing Accountability Act of 2001 and, 124–125
to underage audiences, 58–61, 122
Martin, Kevin, 74
McCarthyism, 111–112

146

"mean world" syndrome, 33

media consolidation, 124

media literacy, 118, 125–126

Media Marketing Accountability Act of 2001 (bill), 124–125

mental illness, 47, 49

meta-analysis, 37

Michigan video game law, 82, 99, 108–109

Miller v. California, 15–16, 17, 21

Miner, Roger, 72

minors. *See also* harmful-to-minors doctrine
amount of television violence witnessed by, 27–28, 61
constitutional rights of, 94–99
fantasy vs. reality and, 28, 34
protection of, 91–94, 111
as victims of violence, 27

Minow, Newton, 56

Miramax Films Corporation v. Motion Picture Association of America, 87, 96–97

moral ambiguity, 75

Morality in Media Inc., 86

Motion Picture Association of America (MPAA), 62, 86–87, 96–97

movies and films
blaxploitation films, 57
Braveheart, 51–52
Clockwork Orange, 55
The Great Train Robbery, 17–18
Hostel, 86–87
increase of violence in, 55
marketing of, 66

Terminator, 78
unrated, 61

Muhammad, John Allen, 54–55

Murphy, Frank, 58

Murray, John, 116–117

music
heavy metal, 36
hip-hop, 57, 72–74, 78
increase in offensive lyrics, 55–56
marketing of, 66–67
Parental Advisory labels on, 20, 62–63, 74
rap, 26

music videos, 20, 38

N

National Association of Broadcasters, 19

National Board of Review, 18

National Commission on the Causes and Prevention of Violence, 120

National Institute of Mental Health, 120–121

National Television Violence Study, 28, 107

NC-17 films, 55, 97

negligence, 105

new media
arrival of age of, 19–22
bias against, 79
as dangerous, 38–39

New York obscenity law, 14, 22–23

news, 110

nighttime hours, channeling of content to, 91, 92–93, 125

O

obscenity
19th-century laws on, 14–15

in *American Amusement Machine Association v. Kendrick*, 102–103
in *Ginsberg v. New York*, 15–16, 20–21, 77
in *Miller v. California*, 15
in *Roth v. United States*, 15, 17
video games and, 80

Olson, Cheryl K., 18, 42, 48–49, 70, 83, 87, 128

P

Pacific Foundation, 110

Parental Advisory Labels, 20, 62–63, 74

parental authority, 68, 106

Parents Music Resource Center, 20

Parents Television Council, 126–127

penny dreadfuls, 79

personal responsibility, 51

Peters, Robert, 86–87

Platform for Internet Content Selection (PICS) system, 122–123

pornographic material, 15–16, 24, 96, 112. *See also* obscenity

Posner, Richard, 80–82, 90, 101, 102–103, 110–111

post hoc ergo propter hoc, 49

Postrel, Virginia, 111, 112–113

Provenza, Eugene, 39

prurient interest, 102

public health, 21–22, 33–38, 118, 121

public opinion, 16–18, 90

R

R rating, 86–87

"race to the bottom," 56

racial bias, 78
racism, 57
Radford, Benjamin,
    46–47
radio, 16, 83, 88–89
Ramos, Charles, 96–97
rap music, 26
ratings systems
    boards, makeup of,
        61, 65
    content-descriptive,
        119
    effectiveness of, 65–67
    European, 87
    increasing leniency
        in, 61
    independent, 126–127
    legal challenges to, 87
    mandatory, 92–93, 123
    movie ratings, 62,
        86–87, 96–97
    music ratings, 62–63
    noncompliance with,
        67, 68
    as sophisticated, 74
    TV ratings, 63–64
    video games ratings,
        64, 125
rational-basis standard,
    21, 77, 98, 117
rational-relationship
    standard, 76
Reason magazine, 111
Recording Industry
    Association of Amer-
    ica (RIAA), 62
Reed, Stanley, 22–23
reflection of violent
    world, 71–74
religious beliefs, 114, 127
Reno v. American Civil
    Liberties Union, 24,
    44–45
replacement of real-
    world violence with
    entertainment, 51–53
research and studies
    AMA resolution, 19

bias in, 42–43
    Centerwall, 28, 32,
        34–35
    contradicted by real-
        world experience,
        44–47
    as flawed, 41–42, 48–51
    interpretation issues,
        116–117
    link between
        entertainment and
        real-world violence,
        29–33, 38–39, 40–41
    longitudinal, 30–31
restraint-of-trade laws,
    123
Rhodes, Richard, 31,
    43, 52
Richardson, Samuel, 16
role-playing games, 128
Rose, Tricia, 57, 60, 71,
    72–74, 78
Rosen, Hilary, 103
Roth v. United States,
    15, 17
Rotunda, Ronald, 43

S

Saunders, Kevin W., 28,
    68, 92–93, 94, 95–97,
    98–99, 117, 122–123
Schechter, Harold, 52–53,
    71, 75, 79, 83–84,
    128–129
school shootings
    Columbine High
        School, Colorado,
        11–12, 47, 117–118
    Virginia Tech
        University, 47, 83
    West Paducah,
        Kentucky, 29, 51, 69,
        104–105
Schwarzenegger, Arnold,
    76, 78
self-regulation. See also
    ratings systems

by entertainment
    industry, 18–19, 21
    as successful, 74–75
    as weak, 61, 67, 122
"Seven Words You Can
    Never Say on Televi-
    sion" (Carlin), 88–89
sexual activity, 46–47
sexual violence, 55, 57
Shakur, Tupac, 26
shooter profile, attempt
    at, 47
Smith, D. Brooks,
    112–113
songs. See music
South Africa, 32
speech, freedom of. See
    First Amendment
    and freedom of
    speech
sports, 110
standards. See legal stan-
    dards
Steinberg, Laurence, 49
stereotyping of black
    men, 57
Stevens, John Paul, 44, 88
Stevens, Robert, 112
strict-scrutiny standard,
    23–24, 45, 76, 98, 117
studies. See research and
    studies
Supreme Court, U.S. See
    also specific cases
    on free speech and
        obscenity, 14–16
    legislation struck down
        by, 24, 44–45
    strict-scrutiny standard
        and, 23–24, 45, 98
Surgeon General's Scien-
    tific Advisory Com-
    mittee on Television
    and Social Behavior,
    120
SWAT 4 (video game),
    75

INDEX

T

television
arrival of, 19, 32, 34–35
and crime rates in 1970s and 1980s, 46
FCC report on, 92–93
homicide rates and, 34–35
increase in violence on, 55
number of violent acts witnessed on, 28
ratings effectiveness, 65–67
ratings system, 63–64
regulation of, 16
self-regulation and, 19
V-chip, 19, 31, 65–67, 126
Television Code, 19, 123
Terminator (film), 78
Thompson, Jack, 69
time spent on media violence, 27–28, 61
tobacco industry, 68, 74–75
trading cards, "true crime," 72–73, 90
"true crime" publications, 14–15, 22–23, 72–73, 87, 90
TV Guardian, 127
TV Parental Guidelines, 63, 74

U

United States v. Stevens, 112–113
unrated films, 61

V

variable obscenity, 20
V-chip, 19, 31, 65–67, 126
victims of violence, children as, 27
Victorian era, 79, 114
video games
as addictive, 38
antisocial behavior and, 57
as beneficial, 83–84
bias against, 82–83
Bully, 57
Columbine High School massacre and, 11–12
desensitization and, 36
Dickerson on, 54
EverQuest, 70
as free speech, 24
Grand Theft Auto, 75, 125
increased violence in, 55
link with violent behavior, 38–39
marketing of, 67
mischaracterization of, 75–76
in public arcades, 80
ratings system, 64, 74, 125
regulation of, 76–77, 80–82, 99, 101, 102–103, 108–109, 125
sexual violence and, 57
suit against makers of, 104–105
SWAT 4, 75
technological advancement in, 20–21

V-Tech Massacre, 110
Woolley suicide and, 70–71
Video Software Dealers Association v. Schwarzeneger, 40–41, 76–77, 103
violence, definition of, 107
Virginia Tech University shootings, 47, 83
V-Tech Massacre (video game), 110

W

Wallace, William, 51–52
War of the Worlds radio drama, 83
WBAI-FM, New York, 88
Wertham, Fredric, 18
West Paducah, Kentucky, shootings, 29, 51, 69, 104–105
Winters, Murray, 22
Winters v. New York, 14, 22–23, 87, 99, 102
women, violence against, 57
Woolley, Shawn, 49, 70–71
World's Fair Torture Chamber (Chicago, 1933), 52–53

X

X rating, 96

Z

Zimring, Franklin, 35

CONTRIBUTORS ||||▷

PAUL RUSCHMANN, J.D., is a legal analyst and writer based in Canton, Michigan. He received his undergraduate degree from the University of Notre Dame and his law degree from the University of Michigan. He is a member of the State Bar of Michigan. His areas of specialization include legislation, public safety, traffic and transportation, and trade regulation. He is also the author of 14 other books in the POINT/COUNTERPOINT series, which deal with such issues as the military draft, indecency in the media, private property rights, the War on Terror, and global warming. He can be found online at www.PaulRuschmann.com.

ALAN MARZILLI, M.A., J.D., lives in Birmingham, Ala., and is a program associate with Advocates for Human Potential, Inc., a research and consulting firm based in Sudbury, Mass., and Albany, N.Y. He primarily works on developing training and educational materials for agencies of the federal government on topics such as housing, mental health policy, employment, and transportation. He has spoken on mental health issues in 30 states, the District of Columbia, and Puerto Rico; his work has included training mental health administrators, nonprofit management and staff, and people with mental illnesses and their families on a wide variety of topics, including effective advocacy, community-based mental health services, and housing. He has written several handbooks and training curricula that are used nationally—as far away as the territory of Guam. He managed statewide and national mental health advocacy programs and worked for several public interest lobbying organizations while studying law at Georgetown University. He has written more than a dozen books, including numerous titles in the POINT/COUNTERPOINT series.